SHELLFISH ON THE GRILL

*More Than 80 Easy and Delectable Recipes
for Lobster, Shrimp, Scampi, Scallops,
Oysters, Clams, Mussels, Crab, and More*

PHYLLIS MAGIDA AND BARBARA GRUNES

Library of Congress Cataloging-in-Publication Data

Magida, Phyllis.
    Shellfish on the grill.

    Includes index.
    1. Cookery (Shellfish).   2. Barbecue cookery.
I. Grunes, Barbara.   II. Title.
TX753.G78   1988   641.6'94   88-7097
ISBN 0-8092-4597-3 (pbk.)

To Lou Green for all his help

Copyright © 1988 by Phyllis Magida and Barbara Grunes
All rights reserved
Published by Contemporary Books, Inc.
180 North Michigan Avenue, Chicago, Illinois 60601
Manufactured in the United States of America
Library of Congress Catalog Card Number: 88-7097
International Standard Book Number: 0-8092-4597-3

Published simultaneously in Canada by Beaverbooks, Ltd.
195 Allstate Parkway, Valleywood Business Park
Markham, Ontario L3R 4T8 Canada

CONTENTS

INTRODUCTION

Shellfish, like other varieties of fish, are low in cholesterol and calories, easy to eat, quick to cook, easy to clean up after, and absolutely delicious. Shellfish, along with fish, are indeed the food of the future.

In this, our second fish grilling book (the first was called *Fish on the Grill*), we have included the most popular types of shellfish eaten in this country. These include the ever popular shrimp, crab, lobster, lobster tails, bay and sea scallops, mussels, oysters, clams, and squid. Besides these popular shellfish, we have also included several recipes for less common types of shellfish, such as conch and snails. And, since barnacles are already a trend on both coasts and are beginning to be eaten in the Midwest, we have included instructions for cooking and eating barnacles as well. You will also find several recipes for frog legs. We know that these are not shellfish—they're amphibians. But since they taste great on the grill, we decided to include them here. We were delighted to discover how well squid works on the grill too—both squid steaks and stuffed squid.

You'll also find some recipes for a new product on the market, sold in supermarket seafood counters and known as imitation crab and lobster. When we experimented with this product, we found it worked very well. And obviously, this and other products like it will be appearing more and more on our tables in the future.

We purposely did not include abalone, whelk, periwinkles, sea urchins, cockles, or limpets in this book because these are not familiar to most people and we felt they did not belong in a book of this size. You will, however, find one recipe for grilled conch, which we included as an oddity.

We can't imagine any vegetable that would not work well on the grill, including some you might not expect to take to this cooking method—okra, turnips (partially cooked to soften somewhat), and salsify. Grilled vegetables are even better if marinated first in Basic Marinade (see Index). Some delicious grilled accompaniments to the shellfish recipes can be found in the last recipe chapter, "Side Dishes on the Grill."

We have combed the planet for the recipes included in this book. Some of the dishes are as much fun to serve as they are to eat, such as Shrimp with Ka'ek and Za'tar. In the Middle East, where *za'tar* (a dried spice mixture) originated, the custom is to snack on hunks of sesame-topped bread called *ka'ek*, dipping them first in olive oil, then in this spice mixture known as *za'tar*. We've added grilled shrimp to this delightful custom and know your guests will enjoy eating shrimp in this manner, as our guests have. Remember, though, when you are serving something unfamiliar, to include something familiar, such as a bowl of hot barbecue sauce or another kind of familiar sauce; you'll find that there is always at least one guest who has trouble with any food that is new.

The portions we suggest in the recipes are more than ample because we know you will appreciate having leftovers. If you wish to decrease the suggested serving amounts, simply ask your fishmonger how much shellfish you'll need for the number of guests you expect.

Before turning to the recipe section, take a few moments to read the information in Part I. There you'll find charts listing the various kinds of seafood and nutritional information on each, information on grills and other tools, and tips for grilling shellfish successfully. If you need instructions on how to get the shellfish out of their shells, before or after grilling, refer to the information at the beginning of each chapter—each type of shellfish has its own chapter in Part II, presented alphabetically.

Happy Grilling,
Phyllis Magida and *Barbara Grunes*

PART I
THE FUNDAMENTALS

1

SHELLFISH FACTS

Shellfish are distinguished from all other kinds of aquatic life by their shells—the hard, external skeletons that give them both structural support and protection, a kind of natural armor, against enemies. This armor ranges in hardness from the easy-to-remove shrimp shells to the oyster and blue crab shells, which are difficult to open.

Shellfish are divided into two classes: crustaceans and mollusks. For culinary purposes, the distinction is simply that the crustaceans (except for the hard-shelled crab varieties) have softer shells and the mollusks harder shells.

Technically, crustaceans are sea animals with hard-crusted bodies that are segmented and joined together by flexible membranes. Crustaceans include American lobsters, crabs, crayfish, shrimp, and spiny lobsters.

Mollusks are more complicated. They're defined as aquatic animals characterized by a calcareous (hard) shell of one or two pieces, enclosing a soft body. What makes them complicated is the fact that they're divided into two classes: univalves (having one valve or shell) and bivalves (having two valves or shells). The univalves we use in this book include conch and snails; squid, too, is a univalve, in which the shell was once present but has been outgrown. The bivalves we use here include clams, mussels, oysters, and scallops.

Whether crustacean or mollusk, bivalve or univalve, the important thing to remember is that all shellfish are accessible, no matter how complicated or hard their shells. Refer to the introductions to each chapter in Part II for directions on opening the shellfish used in this book.

Calories, Protein, and Fat in Shellfish
(3½-oz. raw shelled portion)

SHELLFISH	CALORIES	PRO (g)	FAT (g)
Clams	80	11.0	1.5
Crab, Dungeness	81	17.3	1.3
Crab (imitation), *Surimi* Blend	90	13.4	0.1
Crab, King	75	15.2	0.8
Lobster (1 pound, in shell)	90	16.9	1.9
Lobster, Spiny	74	8.2	1.6
Mussels	75	12.2	1.6
Oysters	70	14.2	1.2
Scallops	82	15.3	0.2
Shrimp	90	18.8	0.8
Squid	85	16.4	0.9

Cholesterol Levels of Shellfish*
(3½-oz. raw shelled portion)

SHELLFISH	CHOLESTEROL (mg)
Abalone	85
Clams	34
Crab, Blue	78
Crab, Dungeness	59
Crab (imitation), *Surimi* Blend	50
Crab, King	42
Crayfish	139
Lobster	70-95
Mussels	80
Oysters, Eastern	55
Scallops	33
Shrimp	152
Squid	233

*Until recently, shellfish was restricted on low-cholesterol diets. It is now known that the types of sterols found in shellfish do not raise blood cholesterol levels and that fish and shellfish are heart-healthy food choices.

Omega-3 Fatty Acids in Shellfish*
(3½-oz. raw shelled portion)

SHELLFISH	OMEGA-3 FATTY ACIDS (g)
Clams	Trace
Crab, Dungeness	0.3
Lobster	0.2
Mussels	0.5
Oysters	0.6
Scallops	0.2
Shrimp	0.3
Squid	0.3

*Because shellfish are lower in fat than most fin fish, there is less of this protective substance than in higher-fat seafoods such as salmon and mackerel. Various studies have shown that omega-3 fatty acids work many ways in the body to help prevent heart disease and cancer.

Sodium Levels in Shellfish*
(3½-oz. raw shelled portion)

SHELLFISH	SODIUM (mg)
Clams	80
Crab, Dungeness	266
Crab (imitation), *Surimi* Blend	600
Crab, King	70
Lobster (1 pound, in shell)	210
Mussels	80
Oysters	75
Scallops	160
Shrimp	140
Squid	160

*Except for imitation crab (*surimi* blend), all shellfish are suitable for use on sodium-restricted diets if sodium is not added in food preparation or in sauces.

2

THE TOOLS: GRILLS, FUELS, AND MORE

In regular indoor cooking, you have to know your oven and your pots and pans. The same holds true in grilling; you have to know your grill, your tools, and your fuel. This chapter will help you familiarize yourself with these elements of grilling.

Minimally, you will need only the simplest equipment: a grill, some fuel, a way to start the fire, and, of course, some shellfish. Maximally, you can have every type of skewer and basket available. You are limited only by your imagination.

GRILLS

There are basically three types of grills, although many variations and attachments appear regularly on the market. All of these are applicable and workable for grilling shellfish, but none are any better than any other, providing you know how to use your grill.

The Basic Brazier

The simplest brazier type consists basically of a pan with raised sides to hold the fire and a grill over the fire to hold the food. It has no

cover to hold in the smoke and no vents to help control the heat. Sometimes it sits on legs; sometimes it's laid flat on the ground. It is manually heated with charcoal, never gas or electricity. This type of grill sometimes costs very little in drugstores and supermarkets. It is very satisfactory for all shellfish (and most other foods). It is not recommended for whole birds and roasts—foods that need longer, slower cooking.

Another type of grill consists of a brazier with a hood. The hood may be merely a shield from the wind and rain, or it can be more elaborate, containing vents to help regulate the heat (shutting off the air helps keep the fire under control), which circulates around the food in a manner similar to the heat circulation in an oven. A cover also increases the amount of smoke circulating around the food, resulting in food with a smokier flavor. It hastens cooking, too, since heat is reflected off the inside surface of the cover.

Round grills with round covers are called *barbecue kettles*. Rectangular grills with rectangular covers (sometimes they have wheels) are often called *grill wagons*. Covered grills most often use charcoal for fuel, though many outdoor cooks today substitute aromatic hardwood chunks or add hardwood to a charcoal base.

A more elaborate type of brazier with a hood is heated by gas or electricity. The heating element is often surrounded by a permanent bed of lava rock or contains a plate to catch the drippings. These grills can be either freestanding or installed permanently in the backyard or on a patio (and, in some cases, in a well-ventilated kitchen or fireplace). When the fat from the food drips onto the bed of volcanic rock, it sizzles and sends up smoke, which helps flavor the food. Some manufacturers of gas and electric grills feel that the smoke from the sizzling fat is wholly responsible for the characteristic barbecue flavor. Our feeling, however, is that the sizzling fat smoke makes up only part of the grilled flavor, that the best grilled food results from a combination of sizzling fat smoke and charcoal and/or wood smoke.

The Hibachi

One ethnic grill, called a Japanese *hibachi*, has become very popular in this country. These cunning little cookers have no legs, which means they can be set up right on the outdoor table where you will be eating. Hibachis are also at their best when set up on fire escapes, back stairs, and rooftops, since they can be easily withdrawn when faced with complaining landlords or neighbors. It's in the nature of the hibachi that it is very small—too small, unfortunately, to make a grilled dinner for four; but it will accommodate two or three adequately. Hibachis can often be quite expensive.

The Water Smoker

The water smoker, a third type of grill, functions differently from the regular charcoal grill. Food put in it to smoke is usually left for several hours—unlike the grilled recipes we suggest in this book, which take only minutes to cook. Water smokers, which consist of a firebox, a pan of water, a grill, and a cover, are at their best when smoking large pieces of food, such as pheasant, duck, turkey, large cuts of meat, and, of course, whole fish. It also accommodates fish steaks or fillets nicely. This grill is perfect for the large fish you catch yourself, bring home, and put on the smoker the same day.

When purchasing a grill, consider the area where you will be cooking. If you have a small balcony, you will need a small grill. With a larger space you have more options. But if you are keen on cooking a lot of shellfish at one time, you may have to juggle the size of the grill with the amount of shellfish you want to cook.

Grilling, whether shellfish or other food, is probably one of the oldest cooking methods. Grill manufacturers have had a lot of time to perfect the equipment, and we recommend all types of grills.

FUEL

Charcoal

There are two basic kinds of charcoal: pure hardwood charcoal, which is sold in lump form, and charcoal that has been compressed into briquet form. Pure hardwood charcoal is made by burning hardwood until it's dry and porous. Pure hardwood charcoal is always marked as such on the box (sometimes with the name of the wood or woods also indicated) and is more expensive than briquets. The smoke that comes from pure hardwood charcoal has a slightly more savory, woody scent and is superior to that from briquets.

Briquets may be labeled simply *briquets, charcoal briquets, compressed wood charcoal,* or something similar. They may be made entirely of charred pieces of wood, or the wood may be compressed mechanically with charred paper and/or sawdust, all of which is held together with some kind of artificial mastic such as a petroleum product. Unfortunately, there is no standard of identity for briquets, so the quality of the smoke they produce when burning varies widely. The best briquets contain very little mastic—just enough to hold them together—and, in the bag, smell faintly of burnt wood. Avoid those that, in the bag, have an artificial odor such as motor oil; these may give off the same odor when they burn. The smoke that comes from burning the best of the impure hardwood briquets is pleasant and acceptable.

In terms of flavor, when grilling shellfish, some people insist it doesn't really matter whether you use pure hardwood charcoal or other kinds of briquets (provided they're of good quality) since shellfish cooks so quickly that it absorbs only a small amount of smoky flavor. Of course, if you're cooking a large, whole fish in a smoker or a covered grill for a long period of time, you may want to use the pure stuff, since a whole fish takes a longer cooking time and so absorbs more smoky flavor.

But for the sake of purity, many people choose pure hardwood charcoal. After all, they reason, fresh shellfish is pure and natural, and grilling is a pure and natural cooking method, so why adulterate the finished product by using impure charcoal? For most of us, good-quality briquets are very acceptable; but if you have a particularly sensitive palate, you'll want to use the pure hardwood stuff.

Aromatics

Whether you use pure hardwood charcoal or plain briquets, you can intensify the smoky flavor of your shellfish by throwing various kinds of aromatics onto your hot coals before cooking. Most aromatics are available in the form of fruitwood or hardwood cuttings and include mesquite, hickory, oak, apple, maple, and cherry wood chips.

Each wood gives its own flavor to the smoke, and you may want to experiment with some of them or mix and match.

Hickory, for example, has a strong, identifiable flavor and a pungent aroma; oak is similar to hickory, but slightly less pungent and a little sweeter. Cherry and other fruitwoods such as apple produce a particularly sweet-smelling smoke and so are effective with more delicately flavored shellfish.

Another wood that recently has gained popularity in America is mesquite, which is available both in hardwood charcoal form and in chip form. At this moment, many restaurants all over America are advertising their "seafood grilled over mesquite," using either the charcoal or a handful of the chips. Thicker, sturdier kinds of fish, such as shark and swordfish, are enhanced by mesquite smoke.

Other common aromatics used in America include stalks of fresh herbs such as thyme, tarragon, basil, fennel, bay leaves, rosemary, sage, and juniper twigs, which can be sprinkled over the hot coals right before setting the shellfish on the grill. (Some buffs tie stalks of fresh herbs into a small bunch, then use this as a basting brush during cooking.) In China, barbecuers throw tea leaves or pieces of orange peel onto the hot coals. And in France, they might substitute grapevine cuttings or a handful of garlic cloves.

Some barbecue buffs enjoy dispensing with charcoal entirely and using just aromatic hardwoods or corncobs as fuel. This is fine for pork or beef. But we do not recommend this with shellfish because the delicate flavor of the shellfish would be overpowered by the strong, assertive fragrances of the smoke given off by some hardwoods alone.

Wood chips should be soaked for several minutes (follow package directions or follow the directions we give in the recipes) before throwing them onto the hot coals, as this will prolong their smoking life. If the chips float when you put them into the pan of water, simply lay a plate over the top to submerge them.

Aromatic woods, charcoal, and other fuels are so widespread that most are available at supermarkets, specialty shops, some hardware shops, and even department stores and pharmacies all over the country. Once you bring your fuel home, store it in a moisture-free area, away from your furnace or heaters.

Electricity and Gas
If you have an electric or gas grill, you can (and should) throw

aromatics onto the bed of lava rock or onto the bottom of the grill. (Remember, we said earlier that the smoke produced by the burning fat of the cooking food is only part of the deliciousness of grilling shellfish; the other part is produced by the smoke from the fuel.) If you do this, though, be sure to turn your grill upside down to shake out the ash at the end of the barbecue season.

MISCELLANEOUS EQUIPMENT

You don't need special equipment for grilling. You can get away with a grill, some charcoal, some starter, a wire brush for cleaning the grill, and a few tools found around any kitchen: a fork, a spatula (the kind used for flipping pancakes), a pastry brush, and a regular pair of kitchen tongs (the kind that were formerly used to handle sterilized baby bottles).

But if you decide to buy special equipment, then we recommend certain types—ones we have found to work very efficiently. A *long-handled fork*, for example, is not only efficient; it also keeps you from burning yourself. And instead of buying a pastry brush, we recommend a *large paint brush* (good quality so the hairs don't come out). A real painter's paint brush is larger, thicker (it will hold more basting butter or sauce), and more efficient than a pastry brush.

Although many *long-handled spatulas*, designed especially for grilling, are available, we recommend those with wide blades. Otherwise, you're better off with a regular kitchen spatula. If you decide to buy *tongs*, buy spring-loaded, stainless-steel tongs. Because they're spring-loaded, they're easier to handle than the ordinary found-around-the-house variety.

There are also special tools available for opening and removing the meat from shellfish. A *clam knife* is a straight-sided knife with a blunt rounded end; the handle should measure four inches in length, the blade two inches to give you good leverage. This size clam knife is used for shucking or opening large quahogs or chowder clams. A smaller knife, similarly shaped, but with a more slender blade, is for opening quahog, cherrystone, or littleneck clams. The flat blade of the clam knife forces the shells apart. The *oyster knife* resembles a clam knife, except it has a sharp curved tip and a round handle. The sharp tip is for getting into the shell, then prying it open.

A *lobster cracker* is a metal tool resembling a nutcracker, used to crack lobster claws. You can substitute a nutcracker. *Lobster shears* look like a pair of metal scissors, strong and short-bladed, made for the purpose of cutting through lobster shells. A metal tool resembling an ice pick, the *lobster pick* is used to remove the meat from narrow lobster claws.

Less common pieces of equipment include *skewers* for shish kabob and *grill baskets*. Skewers can be any length, but avoid those with wooden handles. They look pretty when you buy them, but after a couple of uses the wood finish chars and scorches. Four 10-inch-long all-metal skewers will serve you very well. Eight would be better. If you add an additional eight 20-inch skewers, you'll have all you'll ever need. Whatever size you buy, be sure the skewers are not round. If they are round, the shellfish chunks will slip when you turn the skewer. Each skewer should have four flat sides.

Bamboo skewers are 8- to 10-inch long, narrow bamboo sticks used in the Orient for making skewered foods and are available in Oriental food marts in this country. Bamboo skewers must be soaked in water for 30 minutes prior to using to prevent scorching on the grill.

Grill baskets—wire baskets with covers, which adjust to the shellfish's thickness, attached to long handles—come in a variety of sizes and shapes. Some are rectangular, some are shaped like a fish. The ones we recommend have wires set close together—ideal for grilling sea scallops and shrimp. Grill baskets are useful in turning shellfish. Secured in a basket, the shellfish will not flop around when the basket is turned. If you do use a grill basket, be sure to grease it thoroughly. Baskets can be quite expensive—as high as $20 or more. But if you shop carefully, you should be able to find one for under $12.

You will, of course, be purchasing something with which to start your fire. You can use an *electric starter* (which requires an electric outlet), *a small chimney, a paraffin starter* (a piece of compressed wood or paper with a paraffin base), or the commercial *liquid chemical lighter* available everywhere. But before choosing your starter, be sure to check its aroma. Some chemical starters have an incredibly strong odor that lasts.

3

HOW TO COOK SHELLFISH ON THE GRILL

There is simply no way to judge grilling time for anything so delicate as shellfish, especially when it is exposed to heats so variable as those found on the different kinds and sizes of grills. Grill heat depends on how far the grate is from the coals, whether the grill is gas- or coal-heated, how far along the coals have burned, how thick the shellfish is, and even what the temperature outside may be; if the weather is cold, no matter how hot the grill is, the shellfish being grilled will take a little longer.

In this book we have estimated cooking times based on a grate that is 6 inches from hot coals. However, cooking time lengths can be affected by any or all of the following things: temperature of food (whether it's just been removed from the refrigerator or is at room temperature), temperature of coals, outdoor temperature, thickness and size of the shellfish. The cooking times suggested in this book are intended only as guides. To insure success, you must watch the shellfish carefully as it cooks.

If you need to finish preparing other parts of the meal, you may want to experiment with indirect grilling. In the indirect method, the ashy white charcoal is divided into two small banks on either side of the grill. The shellfish is laid in the center of the grill, away from the direct heat of the charcoal. (Some people lay a pan in the center of the

kettle bottom to catch the drippings.) The shellfish is then cooked—
partly by the heat, partly by the hot smoke. If you cover the grill, the
smoky flavor will be intensified. The advantages of the indirect method
include slow cooking so that you don't have to watch the shellfish quite
so carefully plus maximum exposure to the flavorful smoke.
Disadvantages include a slightly longer cooking time and the necessity
for a cover so that the shellfish will absorb maximum smoke fragrance.

A NOTE ON OYSTER AND CLAM FRESHNESS

Oysters are fresh when their shells remain tightly closed, indicating
the animal inside is alive. If the shells are open and do not close quickly
when you handle them, they should be discarded.

Clams are fresh when their shells remain tightly closed. Like
oysters, if they are slightly open and do not close tightly once they are
touched, they should be discarded. Next, clams should be given the
following test: place them in a large container filled with water and see
if they float; most of them will sink to the bottom, but if any do float,
they should be discarded. Discard also, any clams that have broken
shells.

STARTING A FIRE

Start the fire 45 minutes to an hour before you plan to grill so that
when you are ready to begin cooking, the charcoal will be covered with
a thick layer of grayish-white ash. Pile the briquets into a pyramid in
the center of the grill. An average-size kettle (18–22 inches) needs only
30–35 briquets. Light the charcoal using one of the methods described
in Chapter 2.

How long you'll have to wait before the fire is ready for cooking
depends on a number of factors, but you'll know it's ready when the
charcoal is covered with a fine layer of white ash. At this point, the ashy
charcoal will produce a steady, even heat—perfect for grilling. It is the
direct infrared radiation from the coals that is supposed to do the
major part of the cooking, never a direct flame. If you cook anything,
but particularly shellfish, over flaming coals, you will have trouble
preventing it from burning.

Spread out the briquets, then carefullly brush a little shortening or
oil on the grating if called for in the recipe you're using (don't use
butter—it burns too quickly). And be sure your grill is clean and well
greased. Shelled shellfish have a tendency to stick to a dirty grill.

TIPS FOR COOKING AND SERVING SHELLFISH

1. If shellfish is frozen, defrost it in the refrigerator whenever possible—this will take longer than thawing at room temperature but will keep the shellfish fresh.

2. If possible, buy a grill basket with a narrow grid so that shellfish will not fall through. If you don't have a grill basket, simply skewer the shellfish and cook them, then unskewer them onto the serving platter when cooked. Another alternative is to substitute a bed of seaweed (ask your fishmonger for some) or to lay a sheet of aluminum foil on the grill, then poke it full of holes so that the smoke flavor will permeate the shellfish.

3. Feel free to throw handfuls of any of your favorite fresh herbs on the grill fire, to impart a subtle flavor to the shellfish.

4. *Always* err on the side of undercooking shellfish (see note at the beginning of Part II).

5. Instead of lemon wedges, try substituting lime wedges for sprinkling onto cooked shellfish, as is commonly done in South America.

6. With all of our recipes, if you simply add some white wine or beer, heated French bread with butter, a tossed salad with a vinaigrette dressing, and a bowl of fresh fruit, you'll have a very successful meal.

7. Any leftover cooked fish or shellfish tastes wonderful cold. If desired, make extra by increasing amounts called for in recipes, then chill it and eat the following day.

8. Use only Oriental sesame oil as it has the stronger sesame flavor that is characteristic of many Oriental dishes. Do not use the Middle Eastern variety of sesame oil. It is much lighter in color and will not impart the appropriate flavor to Oriental dishes.

9. Use only Japanese soy sauce as it is thinner, lighter, and less salty than Chinese soy sauce or any other variety. If Japanese soy sauce is not available, thin out the Chinese soy sauce with a little water.

PART II
THE RECIPES

A NOTE ON COOKING SHELLFISH

Shellfish cooking times vary widely, depending on the temperature of the shellfish, heat of the grill, distance of the grill from the heat source, length of marinating time, and thickness and size of shellfish. We cannot stress enough that, when cooking shellfish of any kind, you should watch it carefully. Cook any shellfish until it's just short of being done. It's always better to serve shellfish a tiny bit rare than to risk overcooking it, even a tiny bit. The cooking times indicated in each recipe are the ones that worked for us in that recipe. We were surprised to discover that shrimp put into one marinade often took a shorter time to cook than the same size shrimp put into another marinade.

Once they're on the grill, turn shellfish as desired. In some recipes, we do call for turning the shellfish. In others, we don't. If you watch the shellfish carefully as it cooks, you will know whether or not to turn it.

BASIC MARINADE

½   cup imported good-quality mild olive oil
3   tablespoons fresh lemon juice
2   large cloves garlic, minced fine
¼   teaspoon salt
¼   teaspoon freshly ground pepper
1   bay leaf, crumbled
¼   small onion, cut into chunks (optional)

Mix all ingredients together in a food processor fitted with a steel blade and pulse several times to combine ingredients.

Yield: ½ cup

BARNACLES

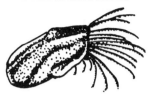

Although we give no recipes for barnacles in this book, they are becoming such a trendy shellfish item on both coasts that we felt we should include instructions for preparing them. Barnacles are crustaceans that taste like a cross between shrimp and lobster. They grow in clusters, each resembling a clump of strange undersea flowers from which five or six stalks protrude. The two- to three-inch stalks—the part that is eaten—are each topped with a tiny mouth that resembles a shell. The stalks are covered with a thick skin, which you pull off as you would pull the paper off a chocolate cigarette.

GRILLED BARNACLES

2 barnacles (per person) as appetizers
Melted butter

Hold the clump of raw barnacles in one hand and break off all of the stalks at the base of the clump. Lay barnacles in a single layer on a heated, well-oiled grill and cook them for 4 minutes on each side. Then examine one barnacle by pulling off skin (directions below). It should have lost its translucent look. If it has not, return it to the grill for a few more minutes.

To eat barnacles: With one hand, pick up a skin-covered stalk. Hold the shell-like mouth section in your left hand. Carefully move your hands in opposite directions against each other to loosen the connection between the skin and the mouth section. Then slip the skin off. You'll see a thin stalk of white meat connected to the shell-mouth section. Dip this in any delicate sauce or melted butter and put the whole thing in your mouth, using your teeth to pull the meat off the inedible portion of the stalk.

CLAMS

Although any of the numerous varieties of this bivalve mollusk will roast well on the grill, we suggest using only the smaller varieties for grilling because the larger ones are tough and best when put into chowders or subjected to slower cooking with moist heat. Hard-shell clams, or quahogs, are most often chopped and used in chowder, while the medium clams, the cherrystones, or the small clams such as littlenecks are used for grilling, steaming, and frying. Clams are available on both the West Coast and the East Coast, but we used New England clams in these recipes.

TO SHUCK CLAMS:

Tool: clam knife. (Note: This is not an oyster knife; a clam knife is a straight-sided knife with a blunt, rounded four-inch blade and a two-inch handle.)

Pick up a clam with one hand and stand it upright, hinge side down, on a pot holder. Hold it tightly with your hand while you insert the clam knife blade between the shells directly opposite the hinge. Once the knife is inserted, begin twisting it and prying open the shells. This may take a couple of minutes.

Another method: Beg your fishmonger to open them for you a short time before you are due to use them in the recipe or substitute canned clams.

BABY CLAM APPETIZER

This recipe for baby clam appetizers can easily be doubled.

EASY SWEET SAUCE

1   12-ounce jar apricot jam
3   tablespoons white vinegar
3   tablespoons water
1   2-ounce jar minced pimiento, drained

SHELLFISH

1   10-ounce can baby clams in water, drained
8   10-inch wooden skewers, soaked in water for 30
    minutes and drained
Oil for greasing grill

    1. *Make sauce:* Combine apricot jam, white vinegar, water, and pimiento in a small saucepan. Heat to boiling point, stirring to combine ingredients. Reduce heat to simmer. Continue simmering for 1 minute. Remove sauce from heat and pour into serving dish. Cool.

    2. *Prepare clams:* Force baby clams onto skewers, jamming them tightly onto the skewers. Brush with sauce. Cover and refrigerate extra sweet sauce for another use.

    3. *Grill clams:* Grill skewered clams on prepared grill over ashen coals for 1½ minutes, being careful not to burn them. Turn skewers and grill an additional minute or until glazed (clams will cook quickly). Arrange decoratively on serving dish and serve hot or warm. Serve two skewers per person.

Yield: 4 servings (1¾ cups sauce)

CLAMS ITALIAN

This dish works nicely on your buffet as an appetizer.

BREADING

4   tablespoons butter
2   cloves garlic, minced
1   small onion, minced
2   teaspoons crumbled dried oregano
1   teaspoon crumbled dried basil
2   cups fine bread crumbs
3   tablespoons grated fresh Parmesan cheese

SHELLFISH

2   dozen medium clams, shucked, bottom shells and any
    juice reserved

1. *Make breading:* Melt butter in large heavy skillet; sauté garlic
and onion over medium heat, stirring occasionally, until onion is soft.
Stir in oregano, basil, and bread crumbs. Blend in ¼ cup of clam juice if
available.

2. *Prepare clams:* Sprinkle 1 tablespoon of breading over each clam
in the shell.

3. *Grill clams:* Arrange clams, open side up, on prepared grill over
hot coals. Cook clams for 8 to 10 minutes. Test one clam to see if ready
to eat. Arrange clams on four individual plates or put on a tray for a
buffet-style dinner. Serve with a small antipasto.

Yield: 4 servings

GRILLED CLAMS ON THE HALF SHELL

TOPPING

6 tablespoons (¾ stick) butter, cut into small pieces
½ teaspoon dried tarragon
½ teaspoon dried fennel seed
¾ cup fine bread crumbs

SHELLFISH

2 dozen medium clams such as topnecks, shucked, leaving clams and some liquid in bottom shells

1. *Prepare topping:* Puree butter, tarragon, and fennel in food processor fitted with steel blade. Blend in bread crumbs.

2. *Prepare clams:* Spoon 1 teaspoon of flavored butter on each clam.

3. *Grill clams:* Arrange clams on prepared grill over ashen coals, about 3 inches from heat source. Cover grill and cook for 2 to 3 minutes or until clams are done to your taste. Serve hot.

Yield: 6 appetizer servings or 4 entree servings

CHEESE-CRUSTED CLAMS

This recipe can easily be doubled.

CHEESE MIXTURE
2   tablespoons butter
½   cup fine bread crumbs
¾   cup grated fresh Parmesan cheese
¼   teaspoon dried thyme
¼   teaspoon dried rosemary
2   egg whites, slightly beaten

SHELLFISH
2   dozen medium clams, shucked
6   10-inch wooden skewers, soaked in water 30 minutes
     and drained
Oil for greasing grill

1. *Prepare cheese mixture:* Melt butter and toss with bread crumbs, cheese, and herbs. Place in a shallow bowl. Pour egg whites into another bowl.
2. Dip each clam in egg whites. Roll in cheese-crumb mixture.
3. *Grill clams:* Thread four clams on one end of each skewer. Grill for 2 minutes on prepared grill over ashen coals. Turn and grill 1 to 2 minutes longer or until clams are done. Serve hot.

Yield: 6 servings

GRILLED CLAMS WITH CORN AND ONION

Aluminum foil
2   dozen medium clams, washed
4   ears corn, shucked and cut into thirds
1   large onion, sliced
¼   pound (1 stick) butter
2   tablespoons fresh lemon juice

1. *Prepare clam packages:* Cut 6 double sheets of aluminum foil large enough to hold four clams and 2 pieces of corn each.

2. Arrange clams, corn, and sliced onion in center of each package. Dot with butter and sprinkle with lemon juice. Seal packages tightly.

3. Arrange packages directly on hot coals. Grill for 3 to 4 minutes, turn packages, and grill 2 to 3 minutes. Test one package to see if it is done. Discard any unopened clams. Serve hot.

Yield: 6 servings

CLAMBAKE, GARLIC BUTTER, AND GRILLED POTATO SKINS

SHELLFISH

2 quarts cold water
¼ cup salt
¼ cup cornmeal
2 dozen cherrystone clams
1½ dozen mussels, cleaned
Enough fresh seaweed to make a bed for shellfish
Oil for greasing grill

GARLIC BUTTER

½ pound (2 sticks) butter, melted
4 cloves garlic, minced
2 tablespoons olive oil
3 tablespoons minced flat-leaf parsley

POTATO SKINS

12 large baking potatoes, baked (see recipe below) and cooled
Peanut oil
Salt to taste
1 cup sour cream
¼ pound bacon, cooked and crumbled
½ cup chopped green onion

1. Soak clams (and mussels if necessary): To rid clams of sand, put 2 quarts water and ¼ cup salt in a large pot. Add clams and sprinkle cornmeal over water. Let clams soak for 1 hour.
2. *Prepare garlic butter:* Pour butter into bowl. Mix in garlic, olive oil, and parsley. Set aside until ready to use.
3. *Prepare potato skins:* Cut baked potatoes in half horizontally. Remove cooled potato pulp, leaving between ¼ and ½ inch of pulp inside skins.
4. Brush outside of potato skins with peanut oil. Cut potatoes in half lengthwise. Sprinkle with salt to taste.

5. *Grill potato skins:* Place potato skins on prepared grill, 3-4 inches away from the coals, and cook for 2 to 4 minutes. Turn over and grill 2 to 4 minutes or until done to taste.

6. *Grill shellfish:* Drain clams and mussels. Make a bed or nest of seaweed on prepared grill. Place shellfish randomly on seaweed. Cover and grill for 10 minutes. Remove cover and discard any unopened shellfish. Serve hot with garlic butter.

7. Serve potato skins hot with sour cream, bacon bits, and chopped green onion.

Yield: 6 servings

BAKED POTATOES

4 medium baking potatoes, about 3½ inches long
Oil for brushing potatoes
Aluminum foil

1. *Prepare potatoes:* Prick potatoes with tines of fork. Brush with oil.

2. *Grill potatoes:* Wrap each potato in aluminum foil. When coals are medium-hot and almost ashen, place potatoes directly on coals. Cook about 30 minutes, turning potatoes twice. Potatoes are done when they feel soft when pierced with a fork. (If you are in a hurry, pierce potatoes with tines of a fork and microwave at high for 4 minutes. Wrap with aluminum foil and cook on coals for about 15 minutes, turning once.)

Yield: 4 servings

CLAM-STUFFED MUSHROOMS ON THE GRILL

MUSHROOMS
24 medium-large fresh shiitake mushrooms

SHELLFISH
2   dozen medium clams, shucked, reserving liquid
1½ cups bread crumbs
1   teaspoon dried oregano
1   teaspoon dried basil
2   cloves garlic, minced
¼   teaspoon salt
¼   teaspoon freshly ground pepper
2   tablespoons butter, melted and cooled
¼   cup grated fresh Parmesan cheese
Oil for greasing grill

1. Remove stems from mushrooms, wipe caps with damp towel, and set aside.

2. *Prepare stuffing:* Toss clams, crumbs, oregano, basil, garlic, salt, and pepper in mixing bowl. Lightly mix in 1 tablespoon liquid from clams, if available, and 2 tablespoons melted butter.

3. Stuff mushrooms lightly with mixture, making sure there is one clam in each mushroom. Sprinkle with Parmesan cheese.

4. *Grill mushrooms:* Arrange mushrooms on prepared grill over ashen coals, about 3 to 4 inches from heat source. Grill mushrooms for 3 to 4 minutes or until just cooked. Serve hot.

Yield: 4 appetizer servings

CONCH

The conch is really a snail—a univalve mollusk. The conch spends most of its life inside a beautiful porcelainlike shell, moving about on a powerful muscular foot, which is, incidentally, the edible portion of the animal. Conch is available fresh, frozen, and canned. If it has not already been tenderized by pounding, it should be pounded with a wooden mallet; otherwise it will be too tough to eat.

TO REMOVE CONCH FROM SHELL:

Removing the live conch from its shell is difficult and unpleasant. A hole must be made in the top of the shell at the third spiral with a hammer; this exposes the muscle that attaches the shell to the body. This muscle must then be cut so that the conch can drop out of its shell. The foot portion should be cut away from the rest of the animal and must then be skinned, pounded, and cut into slices, strips, or chunks.

Another method: We recommend buying it already prepared and frozen, if possible. Once it has been tenderized, conch meat needs only a few moments on the grill on each side. We suggest dipping it in a protective coating before grilling, such as the egg white and bread crumbs we call for in the following recipe.

CONCH ON THE GRILL

Conch is a tough shellfish usually used in soup, but by pounding, breading, and quickly grilling it, you can make it tender and tasty.

BREADING

1½ cups fine bread crumbs
1   teaspoon paprika
½   teaspoon garlic powder
½   teaspoon onion flakes
¼   teaspoon salt
1   egg white, slightly beaten

SHELLFISH

1   pound frozen conch, defrosted in refrigerator or at
    room temperature

1. *Prepare breading:* Toss bread crumbs, paprika, garlic powder, onion flakes, and salt in a shallow dish. Pour egg white into a shallow glass dish.

2. *Prepare conch:* Put conch on waxed paper on a kitchen counter, cut into portion-size pieces and pound with a tenderizer or wooden mallet. Roll in egg white and lightly press on bread crumbs.

3. *Grill conch:* Arrange conch on prepared grill over hot coals and grill 1½ minutes on each side. Some of the crumbs may char or even fall off, but it will not affect the flavor. Serve warm on individual plates. The conch can also be sliced thin and tossed with a pasta salad.

Yield: 4 servings

CRAB

In our testing, we found that fresh crab on the grill tastes best when served with nothing but drawn butter and lemon wedges. So we have not included a recipe for fresh crab, except for the soft-shell variety. If you wish to prepare fresh crab on the grill, ask your fishmonger to prepare the crab for the grill, then take it home and refrigerate. Place it on an oiled, heated grill within two hours and cook it, following directions for grilling lobster (see Index). If you wish to serve a sauce, use any of the sauces given in the chapter on lobster.

TO REMOVE MEAT FROM CRAB SHELL AFTER GRILLING:

Many varieties of crab can be grilled, and the procedure for extracting the meat is basically the same for all of them. Therefore, we've chosen to give directions for the blue crab, one of the hardest-shell varieties. If you wish to remove shells from other varieties of crab, just use these instructions as a guide.

Tools: lobster pick, lobster cracker or mallet.

Once the crab has been grilled, pick it up and look at the underside, locating the apron flap. This is the portion of the shell that grows where the apron would be if the crab were wearing one. Pry off the apron flap, using either your thumb or a knife point. Underneath the apron flap, you will find light green gills on either side of the body. Scrape these out; then scrape out the dark gray digestive organs, which are located in the center of the crab. If you find some orange roe—which means the crab is a female—discard it. Lobster roe is delicious; crab roe is not.

Now turn the crab over and use your thumb or the point of a knife to lift off the top body part of the shell. Then break off the large claws and set them aside. Pick up the crab in both hands and break it in half in the center so the body meat is accessible. Remove the body meat using your fingers or a pick; you can also use a knife. Break off the small legs and throw away unless the crab is so large that the meat in the small legs can be extracted as if you're sipping lemonade through a straw.

To open the large claws on the blue crab, you'll need a lobster cracker or mallet. To use a lobster cracker, insert the claw into the cracker as you would put a nut into a nutcracker. Press down hard. You will probably need to do this in several places on the claw. When the shell is sufficiently broken, pick off the shell pieces. Or, if desired, hit the claw with a mallet. Then use your fingers or the blade of a knife to remove the shell pieces.

SOFT-SHELL CRAB

If you don't want to deal with the shell, but love blue crab, try eating it between the months of May and October. The shell is soft at this time because the crabs have molted.

CRAB LEGS AND CLAWS

Both king crab legs and snow crab claws are available frozen and precooked. It's best to defrost them in the refrigerator. Since they are precooked, grilling time is short.

DUNGENESS CRAB

Dungeness crab is from the Pacific Northwest; it is cooked and then frozen. Each crab averages about 1½ to 2 pounds.

Dungeness crab contains very little meat, and what it does have is honeycombed, making extraction extra difficult. It's so much fun to grill and eat, however, that we do recommend serving it. All you have to do is pretend you are drinking lemonade through a straw.

IMITATION CRAB

Several varieties of imitation crab and lobster are now on the market at prices so much lower than real crab or lobster that we felt this product had to be tested for use in this book. We're happy to report that we found it quite acceptable. If you're troubled by the word *imitation*, don't worry; you're still eating fish. Imitation crab and lobster are made by a Japanese process called *surimi* in which fresh fish is pounded to a paste, flavored, re-formed into a crablike or lobsterlike shape, then cooked. This product is often based on pollack—a saltwater whitefish found in Alaskan waters. The pollack is pounded to a paste, and in many cases the finished product contains 17 percent real crab or lobster, along with lobster or crab shell extracts and flavorings. The *surimi* paste is molded into either crab leg shapes or lobster tail shapes and cooked before being put out in the fish display cases.

Although we do not suggest inviting guests for lobster or crab and then serving them *surimi* products, we do think that these products can be quite good if simply brushed with butter and grilled as imitation crab or lobster.

SOFT-SHELL CRABS WITH PISTACHIO BUTTER

PISTACHIO BUTTER

¼ cup shelled pistachios
¼ pound (1 stick) butter at room temperature
2 tablespoons minced fresh parsley
1 teaspoon fresh lime juice

SHELLFISH

12 soft-shell crabs
Melted butter for brushing crabs
Oil for greasing grill

1. *Prepare pistachio butter:* Blend pistachios and butter in food processor fitted with steel blade. Add parsley and lime juice and combine. Mound pistachio butter in a small bowl, cover, and refrigerate. Remove from refrigerator 45 minutes before serving time so that the pistachio butter will be at room temperature.

2. *Clean soft-shell crabs:* Put crabs, one at a time, on cutting surface. Cut off face portion of crab. Lifting the shell easily on either side of back, scrape off the gills. Lift shell and remove sand receptacle from under the mouth area. Discard all the portions removed from crab. Wash crab and pat dry with paper toweling. Or ask your fishmonger to clean them for you.

3. *Brush crabs with melted butter.* Arrange crabs on prepared grill over hot coals. Grill for 3 minutes. Brush with butter, turn, and continue grilling for 3 minutes or until crabs are a reddish color. Place two crabs on each plate, top with a dollop of pistachio butter while hot, and serve immediately. Pass extra pistachio butter at the table for guests to help themselves.

Yield: 6 servings

SOFT-SHELL CRABS SKEWERED WITH VEGETABLES

VEGETABLES
1 medium zucchini
¾ pound large white mushrooms

SHELLFISH
8 soft-shell crabs
1 tablespoon Hot Cajun Spice
¼ pound (1 stick) butter, melted
4 wooden presoaked Oriental skewers
1 lemon, sliced
Oil for greasing grill

1. *Prepare vegetables:* Cut zucchini into 1½-inch pieces. Trim mushrooms. Set vegetables aside.

2. *Clean soft-shell crabs:* Put crabs, one at a time, on cutting surface. Cut off face portion of crab. Lifting the shell easily on either side of back, scrape off the gills. Lift shell and remove sand receptacle from under the mouth area. Discard all portions removed from crab. Wash crab and pat dry with paper toweling. Or ask your fishmonger to clean them for you.

3. Mix Hot Cajun Spice with melted butter. Brush crabs and vegetables with seasoned butter. Thread vegetables and crabs onto skewers, threading the crabs through the top edge.

4. *Grill crabs:* Arrange skewers on prepared grill over ashen coals and grill for 3 minutes. Brush with seasoned butter, turn over, and continue grilling until crabs are a reddish color, about 3 to 4 minutes longer. Serve hot over fluffy rice or noodles.

Yield: 4 servings

HOT CAJUN SPICE

2   teaspoons cayenne
1   teaspoon ground sweet pepper
2   teaspoons dried minced onion
½   teaspoon garlic powder
¼   teaspoon dried thyme
¼   teaspoon salt
⅛   teaspoon white pepper

Stir all ingredients together until combined.

Yield: about 2½ tablespoons

MESQUITE-GRILLED SPLIT KING CRAB LEGS WITH PICKLED GINGER AND WASABI

WASABI

2   teaspoons cold water
2   tablespoons wasabi powder (see note below)
1   cup (or to taste) pickled ginger (see note below)

SHELLFISH

4   pounds frozen split king crab legs, presliced in half,
     defrosted in refrigerator
3 to 4 4-inch pieces mesquite *or* 2 cups mesquite
     chips, soaked in water 30 minutes and drained
Oil for greasing grill

1. *Prepare wasabi:* Stir 2 teaspoons water with 2 tablespoons wasabi powder in shallow dish until a thick paste is formed. If necessary, add more water, $\frac{1}{2}$ teaspoon at a time. Allow wasabi to stand for 15 minutes and stir.

2. Remove pickled ginger from packet, divide, and mound onto four individual dinner plates. Dollop wasabi next to ginger on plates and set aside.

3. *Grill crab legs:* Arrange mesquite over hot coals and replace prepared grill. Put crab legs cut side down on prepared grill. Cover grill and smoke for 2 to 4 minutes or until crabmeat is flavored to taste. It will have a light brownish smoked appearance.

4. Arrange crab legs on dinner plates and provide a bowl for crab shells.

Note: Wasabi powder (Japanese green horseradish powder) and pickled ginger are available at most Oriental food stores.

Yield: 4 servings

HICKORY-SMOKED KING CRAB LEGS WITH NO-COOK ORANGE SAUCE

NO-COOK ORANGE SAUCE

½ cup orange marmalade
3 tablespoons fresh orange juice
3 tablespoons fresh lemon juice
2 teaspoons prepared white horseradish
¾ teaspoon grated fresh gingerroot
¼ teaspoon salt
2 tablespoons brandy

SHELLFISH

4 pounds frozen king crab legs, presliced in half, defrosted in refrigerator
Melted butter for brushing crab legs
2 cups hickory wood chips, soaked in water for 30 minutes and drained
Oil for greasing grill

1. *Prepare sauce:* Blend all sauce ingredients in a food processor fitted with steel blade or a blender. Place in covered container and refrigerate until ready to serve.

2. *Grill crab legs:* Brush crab legs with melted butter. Sprinkle hickory chips over hot coals and carefully replace prepared grill. Arrange crab legs cut side down on prepared grill. Cover grill and smoke for 2 to 3 minutes or until crabmeat is flavored to taste. It will have a brownish smoked appearance.

3. Serve crab legs with orange dipping sauce.

Yield: 4 servings

SPICY SNOW CRAB CLAWS WITH HORSERADISH SAUCE

HORSERADISH SAUCE
2 cups crème fraîche (see Index)
1 tablespoon prepared red horseradish
1 small red onion, chopped
2 teaspoons fresh lime juice
1 teaspoon fennel seeds

BREADING
1½ cups fine bread crumbs
1 teaspoon paprika
½ teaspoon garlic powder
1½ teaspoons onion flakes
½ teaspoon salt
½ teaspoon crushed red pepper
2 egg whites, slightly beaten

SHELLFISH
2 dozen frozen snow crab claws, defrosted
Oil for greasing grill

1. *Prepare horseradish sauce:* Mix together sauce ingredients and spoon sauce into a serving bowl. Chill until ready to serve.
2. *Prepare breading:* Combine bread crumbs, paprika, garlic powder, onion flakes, salt, and crushed red pepper in a shallow bowl or pie plate. Pour egg whites into a shallow dish.
3. Roll exposed crab section in egg whites and then in crumb mixture. Put paper toweling in bottom of cookie sheet and place crab claws on the paper.
4. *Grill crab claws:* Arrange claws across grid of prepared grill, about 3 to 4 inches from heat source, and grill for 2 minutes. Turn crab claws over and grill for 1 to 2 minutes or until done.
5. Serve on individual plates with horseradish dipping sauce.

Yield: 4 servings

DUNGENESS CRAB WITH SHALLOT BUTTER AND GRILLED SHALLOTS

SHALLOT BUTTER

3   medium shallots
¼   pound (1 stick) butter
2   tablespoons heavy cream
½   teaspoon crumbled dried thyme
1   teaspoon crumbled dried green peppercorns
2   medium shallots (for grilling)

SHELLFISH

4   1½-pound frozen Dungeness crabs, defrosted in
    refrigerator or at room temperature
Oil for greasing grill

1. *Prepare shallot butter:* Puree 3 peeled shallots in food processor fitted with steel blade. Blend in butter. Add cream, thyme, and green peppercorns; mix all ingredients together. Spoon into a small bowl, cover, and refrigerate. Bring to room temperature before serving.

2. Arrange remaining shallots, with skins on, at outer edge of ashen coals. Cook for 8 minutes, turn, and continue cooking for 3 to 4 minutes or until soft. The outer wrapping may char. Place shallots on serving dish.

3. *Grill crabs:* Put crabs, shell side up, on prepared grill and grill for 3 to 4 minutes. Turn crabs over and grill 1 to 2 minutes longer. The crabs will turn red. Place crabs on serving dish.

4. Serve crabs hot with shallot butter and roasted shallots. Squeeze warm shallots out of skin and eat with vegetables or on roasted potatoes or tomatoes. Serve crabs with picks. There isn't much meat, but it is lots of fun.

Yield: 4 servings

MARYLAND-STYLE CRAB CAKES ON A BED OF PARSLEY

MUSTARD SAUCE

½ cup mayonnaise
¾ cup sour cream
1 teaspoon dry mustard
2 teaspoons prepared rough-grained mustard

CRAB CAKES

1 pound crabmeat, picked over, cartilage discarded, and any liquid squeezed out
¼ cup fine bread crumbs
1 egg, beaten
1 tablespoon mayonnaise
½ teaspoon (or to taste) Worcestershire sauce
½ teaspoon dry mustard
½ teaspoon salt
¼ teaspoon white pepper
3 tablespoons minced fresh parsley
All-purpose flour
2 eggs, slightly beaten
Bread crumbs
Oil for greasing grill
2–3 cups parsley sprigs

1. *Prepare mustard sauce:* Stir together sauce ingredients; place in a covered container, and refrigerate until needed.

2. *Prepare crab cakes:* Combine ¼ cup fine bread crumbs, egg, mayonnaise, Worcestershire, mustard, salt, pepper, and parsley in a deep bowl. Form into six firm patties.

3. Roll patties in flour, then dip into the beaten eggs. Roll in bread crumbs.

4. *Grill crab cakes:* Spread parsley as a nest on prepared grill. Arrange patties over parsley. Or you can grill the crab cakes in a grill basket. Cook for 3 to 4 minutes over medium-hot coals. Turn patties with spatula and grill 3 minutes longer or until done. Serve hot with mustard sauce.

Yield: 4–6 servings

MOCK CRAB SALAD SANDWICHES

The mesquite smoke imparts a wonderful flavor to the mock crab.

FISH
1   pound mock crab legs
Melted butter for brushing crab legs
3 to 4 4-inch pieces mesquite *or* 2 cups mesquite
    chips, soaked in water 30 minutes and drained
Oil for greasing grill

SALAD
6   ounces mild goat cheese, cut into ½-inch chunks
1   cup chopped walnuts
½   cup chopped fresh chives
6   tablespoons (¾ stick) butter, melted
Best-quality white bread

1. *Grill crab legs:* Brush crab legs with melted butter and set aside. Arrange mesquite on hot coals and replace grill carefully. Set crab legs on prepared grill, cover, and cook for 2 minutes. Remove cover, turn legs over, and continue cooking for 2 minutes.

2. Remove crab legs, cool, and chop them into ¾- to ½-inch chunks; place in deep mixing bowl. Toss crab with goat cheese, walnuts, chives, and 6 tablespoons melted butter. Prepare sandwiches on best-quality fresh bread.

Yield: 6–8 sandwiches

MARINATED MOCK CRAB LEGS WITH PASTA

MARINADE
1 cup virgin olive oil
¼ cup red wine vinegar
½ teaspoon paprika
½ cup chopped green onion

FISH
1¼ pounds mock crab legs
3 to 4 4-inch pieces mesquite *or* 2 cups mesquite
   chips, soaked in water 30 minutes and drained
Oil for greasing grill

PASTA SALAD
¾ pound spiral noodles, cooked according to package
   directions
1 cup sliced celery
1 small red onion, chopped
2 tomatoes, peeled, seeded, and chopped
2 teaspoons crumbled dried basil
½ teaspoon salt
¼ teaspoon freshly ground pepper
½ cup sour cream
½ cup mayonnaise

1. *Prepare marinade:* Combine marinade ingredients in a shallow bowl or glass pie plate. Marinate crab legs for 30 minutes, turning once.

2. *Grill crab legs:* Arrange mesquite on hot coals and carefully replace grill. Set crab legs on prepared grill, cover, and cook for 2 minutes. Remove cover and turn legs over; they will tend to separate, so turn carefully with a spatula. Continue cooking for 1 to 2 minutes.

3. Remove legs and chop into ¾- to ½-inch chunks; place in deep mixing bowl. Toss crab with drained, cooled pasta, celery, onions, and tomatoes. Season with basil, salt, and pepper. Stir in sour cream and mayonnaise. Arrange on individual plates or use as a buffet item.

Yield: 6 servings

CRAYFISH

For cooking purposes, this variety of crustacean should be considered a small lobster, since it is covered with a similar shell and resembles a lobster. Crayfish are usually anywhere between three and eight inches in length. Ask the fishmonger to prepare these animals for grilling just as you would ask him to prepare lobsters. Then take them home, refrigerate, and cook them within two hours. Grill crayfish in their shells, using a grill basket if possible, or skewer them.

In summer, during crayfish season, the Finnish people consume an unbelievable amount of crayfish, which they boil in highly flavored water instead of putting them on the grill. The crayfish are then allowed to steep in this water until they're ready to eat. We prefer them grilled and flavor them by serving a highly seasoned dill butter with them. The Finns, who eat crayfish tails cold, say that custom dictates that a drink of aquavit, beer, or white wine be taken with each tail. Certainly, if you follow this dictum, it should make for a lively, uninhibited party.

TO REMOVE CRAYFISH SHELLS:

After grilling, pick up the crayfish, holding the tail in one hand and the head in the other. Twist your hands in opposite directions and pull the crayfish apart. Hold the body to your lips, drawing in the juices as if you were sucking on a straw. Then pry the tail open with your fingers to extract the meat, using your thumb as a lever.

GRILLED CRAYFISH FINNISH STYLE

You may want to serve aquavit and rye bread with this recipe and follow dinner with a dessert of fresh berries in season and sweetened whipped cream.

DILL BUTTER
¼ pound (1 stick) butter
¼ cup minced fresh dill
3 tablespoons aquavit
1 teaspoon dill seeds

SHELLFISH
6 pounds crayfish, prepared for grilling by fishmonger
Oil for greasing basket
2 cups fresh dill

1. *Prepare dill butter:* Melt butter in small heavy saucepan over low heat. Stir in dill, aquavit, and dill seeds. Pour dill butter into serving dish.

2. *Grill crayfish:* Rinse crayfish. Arrange in prepared hinged grill basket or on grill. Cover crayfish with ¾ cup fresh dill sprigs and secure basket. Unless you have two or more grill baskets, it will be necessary to repeat procedure until all the crayfish have been grilled. Put basket on grill over hot coals 3 to 4 inches from heat source. Grill 2 to 3 minutes, turn basket, and grill 2 minutes longer. Crayfish will turn a bright red.

3. Scatter remaining dill on a large platter. Mound crayfish in the center over dill. Serve hot or cool with dill butter as a dipping sauce. Guests open their own crayfish. Provide a bowl for shells. To eat crayfish, see directions at the beginning of this chapter.

Yield: 6 servings

FROG LEGS

Frogs are not shellfish at all; they are amphibians with long hind legs adapted for jumping. But they're so often put into this category gastronomically that we decided to include them in this book. Frog legs taste like a combination of lobster and chicken. They are commercially grown and marketed all over the United States and are available frozen in many supermarkets. Although they come in small, medium, and large sizes, we suggest buying only the smallest and most tender you can find.

FROG LEGS WITH TROPICAL FRUIT

FRUIT SAUCE
1 cup mashed mango pulp
½ cup sweetened flaked coconut
¼ cup crushed pineapple with juice
2 teaspoons fresh lime juice

SEAFOOD
12 pairs frozen frog legs, defrosted in refrigerator or at room temperature
¾ cup chili sauce
3 green onions, minced
Oil for greasing grill

1. *Prepare fruit sauce:* Combine sauce ingredients in a bowl and stir together until blended. Cover and refrigerate until needed.

2. *Prepare frog legs:* Wash legs and pat dry; arrange in a shallow glass pan. Stir together chili sauce and onions. Brush frog legs with chili sauce and let stand for 20 minutes.

3. *Grill frog legs:* Place frog legs on prepared grill over ashen coals about 3 to 4 inches from heat source. Grill 3 to 4 minutes. Brush with extra sauce. Turn and continue grilling for 2 minutes or until legs are cooked. Serve hot with hot rice and fruit sauce.

Yield: 6 servings

FROG LEGS ORIENTAL

This recipe yields two pairs of frog legs per person, but sometimes three pairs are considered a serving, so grill more if you wish.

HOISIN SAUCE MIXTURE
1   cup hoisin sauce (see note below)
1   teaspoon soy sauce
1   teaspoon sugar
2   teaspoons Oriental sesame oil

SEAFOOD
12 pairs frozen frog legs, defrosted in refrigerator or at
      room temperature
Oil for greasing grill

1. *Prepare hoisin sauce mixture:* Combine sauce ingredients in small heavy saucepan. Cook over low heat until hot. Cool, cover, and refrigerate until needed. Reheat before serving.
2. *Grill frog legs:* Brush with hoisin sauce mixture and grill on prepared grill over ashen coals for 3 minutes. Flip frog legs and again brush with hoisin sauce mixture and continue grilling for 2 to 3 minutes or until done. Serve hot with extra hoisin sauce mixture at the table, along with hot rice or noodles.

Note: Hoisin sauce is available at Oriental food markets and some large supermarkets.

Yield: 6 servings (with 1 cup sauce)

FROG LEGS WITH PESTO SAUCE

Pesto is best prepared in late summer when fresh basil is plentiful. This sauce freezes very well.

PESTO SAUCE

½ cup pine nuts
2 cloves garlic, peeled
2 cups fresh basil leaves
¼ teaspoon salt
½ cup grated fresh Parmesan cheese
1 cup good-quality olive oil

SEAFOOD

12 pairs frozen frog legs, defrosted in refrigerator or at
    room temperature
Oil for greasing grill

1. *Prepare pesto sauce:* Puree pine nuts and garlic in food processor fitted with steel blade. Add basil and puree. Mix in salt and cheese. With the machine still running, add oil in a slow, steady stream until it is incorporated. Place sauce in a covered container and refrigerate until needed.

2. *Grill frog legs:* Brush frog legs with pesto sauce and place on prepared grill. Cook for 3 minutes. Brush again with pesto sauce and turn over. Continue grilling for 3 minutes or until done. Serve frog legs hot with a pasta dish.

Yield: 6 servings (with 1½ cups sauce)

FROG LEGS WITH BARBECUE SAUCE AND GRILLED TOMATILLOS

BARBECUE SAUCE

3 tablespoons butter
3 green onions, chopped
2 cloves garlic, minced
½ cup chili sauce
¼ cup catsup
1 tablespoon Gebhardt chili powder, or a good quality chili powder
½ teaspoon Worcestershire sauce
1 teaspoon prepared mustard
3 drops (or to taste) hot pepper sauce

SEAFOOD AND TOMATILLOS

8 tomatillos (see note below)
Oil for greasing grill and tomatillos
12 pairs frozen frog legs, defrosted in refrigerator or at room temperature

1. *Prepare barbecue sauce:* Heat butter in medium saucepan and sauté onions and garlic in it only until tender. Mix in remaining sauce ingredients. Simmer for 10 minutes, stirring occasionally. Cool.

2. Brush tomatillos with oil, leaving outer skin in place. Set aside.

3. Arrange frog legs in a glass dish and cover with barbecue sauce. Marinate for 1 hour, turning once.

4. *Grill frog legs:* Place frog legs on prepared grill and cook for 3 minutes. Brush with sauce, turn over, and continue cooking for 2 minutes or until done.

5. *Grill tomatillos:* Cut tomatillos in half, brush with oil again, and grill cut side up for 2 minutes. Turn over and grill 2 minutes or until done. Serve frog legs with tomatillos.

Note: Tomatillos are readily available in most of the larger supermarkets, as well as in Mexican and Cuban food stores.

Yield: 6 servings (with 1 cup sauce)

FROG LEGS WITH SHIITAKE MUSHROOMS AND HERBS ON THE GRILL

Shiitake mushrooms are available at many gourmet markets and by mail order (see Appendix). Store mushrooms in refrigerator, covered loosely with a damp cloth and not in a plastic bag.

SHIITAKE MUSHROOMS
½ pound fresh shiitake mushrooms
Melted butter for brushing mushrooms
½ cup dried rosemary
½ cup dried thyme

MARINADE
½ cup good-quality olive oil
3 tablespoons fresh lemon juice
3 tablespoons minced fresh parsley
½ teaspoon garlic powder

FROG LEGS
12 pairs frozen frog legs, defrosted in refrigerator or at
    room temperature
Oil for greasing grill

1. *Prepare mushrooms:* Remove and discard stems. Wipe caps with damp towel. Brush mushroom caps with melted butter. Sprinkle with 3 tablespoons each of rosemary and thyme and set aside.

2. *Prepare marinade:* Combine marinade ingredients in a shallow glass bowl. Marinate frog legs for 1 hour, turning once, and drain, reserving marinade.

3. *Grill mushrooms and frog legs:* Sprinkle remaining herbs over hot coals. Working quickly, put mushroom caps (cap side down) and frog legs on prepared grill. Cover and cook for 3 minutes. Remove mushrooms, brush frog legs with marinade, turn over, and continue grilling for 2 to 3 minutes or until done. Serve mushrooms with frog legs.

Yield: 6 servings

LOBSTER

The American lobster, a crustacean, is also called the *Maine lobster* and is distinguished by its two large claws called the *crusher* claw and the smaller *quick* claw. Hard-shelled lobsters are preferred because they contain more meat, and female lobsters are also favored because of the roe.

TO PREPARE LOBSTERS FOR GRILLING:

We strongly urge you to have the fishmonger do all the preparation of the lobster for the grill, since his manner is both quick and painless to the lobster. Once you've picked up the prepared lobster, take it home quickly and refrigerate, then grill it within a couple of hours. Lobsters can be put whole on the grill, once the fishmonger has prepared them.

Or you can ask your fishmonger to do the following pregrilling preparation: Split the lobster lengthwise, cutting through the top shell and meat, but not cutting through the bottom shell. Then, open the lobster to butterfly it and remove and discard the stomach and white intestinal vein.

If you have had experience with preparing lobsters and feel that you can do it yourself, buy them live (you may store them in the refrigerator for one to two days). Place the lobster on its back, protect your hands with a towel, and with a very sharp, strong knife, make a deep slit from thorax to tail, cutting the lobster in half lengthwise without cutting through the bottom shell. Open the lobster to butterfly it and remove and discard the stomach and the white intestinal vein. Green tomalley and roe can be left in place.

TO REMOVE SHELL FROM WHOLE GRILLED LOBSTER:

Tools: lobster cracker, lobster pick.

Pick the lobster up in one hand and locate a claw—one of the big arms that resemble big red boxing gloves. Use your other hand to twist this claw from the body. Then twist off the second claw in the same manner. Pick up the lobster cracker (the tool that resembles a nutcracker) in your right hand, insert one of the lobster claws into it, and press down hard until the shell breaks. Use the lobster cracker on various sections of the claw until the shell is sufficiently broken. Then remove as much of the shell as possible with your fingers and eat the meat. Repeat with the remaining claw.

Next, pick up the whole lobster, holding the tail in one hand and the body/head section in the other, and crack the lobster in half so that you end up with one section in each hand. Lay the tail section down and hold the body/head section belly side up. Stick your right thumb between the meat and the shell bottom and lift, using your fingers to pull the meat out of the shell. Break off the tiny claw-legs still connected to the body meat you've removed and reserve them for a moment. Then remove the second, softer undershell, call the *belly shell.*

Next, discard the black vein that runs the length of the body meat. You should also discard the small sac at the base of the lobster's head called the *sand sac.* Everything else—including the tomalley (drab green-colored liver)—is safe to eat. You may even find some coral-colored roe (eggs), if your lobster is female. Both the tomalley and the roe are delicious.

Finally, pick up the tail section in one hand. Use the other hand to bend the tail section back and break the flippers off the end. Insert a lobster fork into the hole you've made and push gently; the tail meat will come out the other end. When it does, remove the black vein that runs the length of the tail and discard.

To eat the small claw legs, put the open end of each into your mouth, and suck out the meat as if using a straw.

LOBSTER TAILS

Lobster tails are harvested from both warm and cold waters. The warm areas are the Caribbean, Mexican, and South African waters; the cold-water tails are from New Zealand and Australia. Cold-water tails seem to have a firmer texture and somewhat sweeter taste.

Lobster tails come mostly from a crustacean known as the *spiny lobster* or *langouste,* as it is called in France, which hails from as far away as South Africa, Australia, and the Mediterranean or as close as Florida and California. They also come from miniature lobsters, similar to the spiny, which are found in the deep waters of the Adriatic Sea and are marketed in this country as deep-sea tails (the Italians call those deep-sea tails *scampi*). Spiny lobsters have no large claws, so they are most conveniently sold as tails—that is, without even the tiny clawlike appendages they possess.

In America, lobster and deep-sea tails are usually sold frozen in sizes ranging from three ounces to over two pounds each. The best way to defrost them is slowly, uncovered, in the refrigerator or at room temperature. Always defrost them before grilling.

TO PREPARE LOBSTER TAILS FOR GRILLING:

Simply use a sharp knife or kitchen shears to cut away the top membrane, then use the knife to loosen the lobster meat from the shell, taking care to leave the shell partially connected.

MONKFISH—POOR MAN'S LOBSTER

Monkfish is often referred to as "poor man's lobster," so we're including three recipes for it in this chapter. The nickname is apropos; monkfish certainly costs less than lobster. And it resembles lobster texturally, although the two have different flavors: lobster's flavor is delicate, but monkfish has a blander, less sweet taste. You can minimize this defect by serving monkfish with a strong-flavored sauce. (And incidentally, monkfish tastes more like lobster when cold.) Don't limit yourself to the sauces we suggest for monkfish. Many strong-flavored sauces would be equally good with monkfish.

A word of caution: examine monkfish fillets carefully, making sure they are thoroughly skinned. Look particularly at the ridge area down the center. If any skin remains in this ridge, it will make the fish tough.

When cooking monkfish, if one end is much thicker than the other, butterfly that section only to ensure more even cooking. Do this before putting it in the marinade.

WHOLE LOBSTERS WITH VANILLA SAUCE A LA CHEF THIERRY LEFEUVRE

Thierry LeFeuvre is the talented young chef-owner of Froggy's Cafe, 306 Green Bay Road, Highwood, Illinois.

VANILLA SAUCE
2 teaspoons butter
3 shallots, minced
4 tablespoons dry white wine
1 vanilla bean, slit
3 cups heavy cream
¾ pound bay scallops
⅛ teaspoon salt
⅛ teaspoon white pepper

SHELLFISH
6 Maine lobsters, 1¼–1½ pounds each, prepared for grilling
Melted butter

1. *Make vanilla sauce:* Melt 2 teaspoons butter in a medium saucepan over low heat. Sauté shallots for 3 minutes or until tender, stirring often. Stir in white wine and vanilla bean. Mix well and cook over medium-high heat until mixture is almost dry. Stir in cream and bring mixture to a boil. Reduce heat and simmer about 3 minutes. Add scallops, salt, and white pepper and continue cooking until scallops are just cooked. Remove scallops. Strain sauce and return scallops. Set aside. Keep warm.

2. *Grill lobsters:* Using a pastry brush, brush cut sides of prepared lobsters with melted butter. Arrange lobsters shell side up on prepared grill, 3 to 4 inches from ashen coals, and cook for 6 to 8 minutes. Brush with butter, turn lobsters over, and continue grilling for 2 minutes or until done. Lobster is cooked when the meat is opaque and it starts to separate from shell. *Do not overcook lobsters.* Serve lobsters on top of warm sauce.

Yield: 6 servings (with about 3 cups sauce)

WHOLE MAINE LOBSTERS HOT FROM THE GRILL WITH LEMON BUTTER OR CHILLED WITH HERB MAYONNAISE

Prepare only one of the two sauces below—lemon butter if you plan to serve the lobsters hot from the grill or herb mayonnaise if you wish to serve the lobsters cold.

LEMON BUTTER
$\frac{1}{4}$ pound (1 stick) butter at room temperature
1 tablespoon fresh lemon juice
1 tablespoon finely grated lemon zest
1 tablespoon finely minced fresh parsley
Dash hot pepper sauce

HERB MAYONNAISE
2 egg yolks at room temperature
2 tablespoons red wine vinegar
1 tablespoon Dijon mustard
1 tablespoon chopped fresh parsley
1 tablespoon chopped fresh tarragon
$\frac{1}{4}$ teaspoon salt
1 cup olive oil

SHELLFISH
4 Maine lobsters, about $1\frac{1}{4}$–$1\frac{1}{2}$ pounds each
Melted butter
Oil for greasing grill
Lemon slices for garnish

1. *Prepare lemon butter:* Soften $\frac{1}{4}$ pound butter in food processor fitted with steel blade or in a bowl using the back of a wooden spoon. Stir in lemon juice, lemon zest, 1 tablespoon parsley, and hot pepper sauce. Spoon into a serving dish and refrigerate. Bring to room temperature 45 minutes before serving.

2. *Prepare herb mayonnaise:* Put egg yolks in food processor or blender container along with red wine vinegar, mustard, 1 tablespoon parsley, tarragon, and salt. Process for about 5 or 6 seconds or as necessary to combine.

3. With motor running, begin adding the oil in a slow, steady stream. Keep motor running until all oil is added, then turn off machine. Let mayonnaise sit at room temperature for 5 minutes before serving. Cover any leftover mayonnaise; it will keep from 1 to 2 days in refrigerator.

4. *Grill lobsters:* Using a pastry brush, brush cut sides of prepared lobsters with melted butter. Arrange lobsters shell side up on prepared grill, 3 to 4 inches from ashen coals, and cook for 6 to 8 minutes. (Grilling shell side up prevents loss of juice.) Brush with butter, turn lobsters over, and continue grilling for 2 minutes or until done. Lobster is cooked when the meat is opaque and it starts to separate from shell. Do not overcook lobsters.

5. Serve lobsters hot with lemon butter or chilled with herb mayonnaise. Garnish with lemon slices. Give each diner a disposable bib, a lobster cracker, a pick, and a damp finger towel.

Yield: 4 servings (with 1 cup lemon butter or 1⅔ cups herb mayonnaise)

SPINY LOBSTER WITH EASY CREAMY ROQUEFORT SAUCE

Spiny lobsters are usually shipped frozen and should be defrosted in the refrigerator or at room temperature before using. The color of the lobster can vary from a dark red to a mottled color with or without spots. The meat tends to be somewhat softer in texture and slightly less sweet than the meat of the cold-water tails.

ROQUEFORT SAUCE
2½ cups heavy cream
6–8 ounces Roquefort or other veined cheese, crumbled
3   tablespoons minced fresh chives

SHELLFISH
6   1¼-pound frozen spiny lobsters, defrosted
Oil for greasing grill
Melted butter for brushing lobster tails

1. *Make Roquefort sauce:* Warm cream in medium saucepan over low heat. Mix in cheese and chives and simmer for 1 minute. Remove from heat.

2. Cut and remove membrane from center to tail. Cut away underpart of lobster without disconnecting from shell completely.

3. Arrange lobsters cut side up on prepared grill over medium-hot ashen coals about 3 to 4 inches from coals. Brush with melted butter. Grill about 6 minutes. Bottom of lobster shell may char. Brush lobster meat with butter, turn over, and grill for 1 to 2 minutes or until meat is opaque and pulling away slightly from sides of shell.

4. Place lobster on individual plates and serve with warm Roquefort sauce. Place disposable bibs, nutcrackers, and picks at table around place settings. Serve damp finger cloths after dinner.

Yield: 6 servings

LOBSTER TAILS WITH NEWBURG BUTTER

Sometime in the 1890s, Delmonico's, a famous restaurant in New York, decided to bestow the ultimate honor upon one of its customers and name a dish after him. The customer—Benjamin Wenberg—had been such a frequent customer at the restaurant that Mr. Delmonico decided to call a special lobster dish Lobster Wenberg. Unfortunately, Delmonico and Wenberg had a bitter quarrel from which the friendship did not recover. Delmonico soon renamed the dish Lobster Newburg, which is the name used today.

NEWBURG BUTTER
¼ pound (1 stick) butter, cut into chunks
3 tablespoons heavy cream
4 tablespoons sherry
¼ teaspoon grated nutmeg

SHELLFISH
4 frozen lobster tails, 12–14 ounces each, defrosted
Melted butter for brushing lobster tails
Oil for greasing grill

1. *Make Newburg butter:* Puree ¼ pound butter in a food processor fitted with steel blade. Incorporate cream and mix in sherry and nutmeg. Mound butter in serving dish, cover, and refrigerate. Bring to room temperature before serving.

2. *Grill lobster tails:* Cut and remove outer membrane from lobster tails. Brush with melted butter. Arrange tails cut side up on prepared grill over ashen coals, about 3 to 4 inches from heat. Grill for 8 to 10 minutes. Lobster meat will turn from translucent to opaque during cooking. Turn lobster tails over and continue cooking for 2 to 3 minutes or until lobster is cooked. Shells may char on bottom.

3. Place a tail on each plate and spread soft Newburg butter over hot lobster meat. Pass extra butter at table for guests to help themselves.

Yield: 4 servings

FLAMING LOBSTER TAILS WITH LEMON-LIME MARINADE

The effect of flaming at the table is very dramatic, but this recipe can be prepared without flaming if you wish.

MARINADE

¼ pound (1 stick) butter, melted and cooled
2 tablespoons fresh lemon juice
2 tablespoons fresh lime juice
1 tablespoon grated lime zest
2 bay leaves
2 cloves garlic, minced
2 bay leaves
¼ teaspoon white pepper

SHELLFISH

6 frozen lobster tails, 10–12 ounces each, defrosted at room temperature
Oil for greasing grill
3 ounces brandy

1. *Make marinade:* Combine marinade ingredients in a shallow glass bowl or pie plate.
2. Cut away and remove the membrane from top of lobster tails. Partially loosen meat from shell but leave connected. Arrange lobster tails cut side down in marinade and marinate for 1 hour. Drain, reserving marinade.
3. *Grill lobster tails:* Arrange lobster tails cut side up on prepared grill over ashen coals, about 4 inches from heat. Cook 8 minutes. Brush with reserved marinade and turn over. Continue grilling for 2 minutes or until tails are cooked. Lobster meat will be opaque.
4. Remove tails from grill to a flameproof serving dish. Bring to table cut side up. Heat brandy and pour over tails. Carefully ignite brandy. Wait until flame burns out, about 1 minute, and serve.

Yield: 6 servings

STUFFED LOBSTER TAILS

STUFFING

2 tablespoons butter
4 tablespoons chopped fresh chives
2 tablespoons chopped fresh parsley
¼ teaspoon salt
⅛ teaspoon freshly ground pepper
1½ cups bread crumbs

SHELLFISH

6 frozen lobster tails, about 10 ounces each, defrosted at
   room temperature
Melted butter
Oil for greasing grill

1. *Prepare stuffing:* Melt 2 tablespoons butter in medium frying pan. Add chives and sauté over low heat, stirring, for 2 minutes. Add parsley, salt, and pepper. Remove from heat. Stir in bread crumbs, mixing well.

2. With kitchen shears, cut top membrane off lobster tails and discard. Partially loosen meat from shell, leaving tail section connected. Brush lobster tails with melted butter.

3. Lightly pack stuffing into cavity between the meat and the shell.

4. *Grill lobster tails:* Arrange tails shell side down on prepared grill, 3 to 4 inches from heat source, and cook for 8 to 10 minutes. Brush with butter, turn over, and continue cooking for 2 to 3 minutes or until lobster is cooked. Meat will be opaque and firm. Serve with melted butter.

Yield: 6 servings

POOR MAN'S LOBSTER WITH GREEN CHILE SAUCE

SEAFOOD

2 pounds monkfish fillets
1 recipe Basic Marinade (see Index)
Oil for greasing grill

GREEN CHILE SAUCE

2 medium onions, quartered
3 4-ounce cans mild green chilies, chopped and drained
1–2 canned jalapeño peppers, packed in vinegar,
  water, and salt (do not use oil-packed) *or*
  1–2 fresh jalapeños, seeded
2 tablespoons butter
¾ teaspoon salt
½ cup half-and-half, heated (do not let boil)

1. Place monkfish in a plastic bag and set in a bowl. Pour marinade into bag and secure with twister seal. Turn bag a couple of times to be sure all fish surfaces touch marinade. Let sit at room temperature 1 hour.

2. *While monkfish marinates, prepare sauce:* Place quartered onions in food processor fitted with steel blade and pulse several times until coarsely chopped. Add drained green chilies and jalapeño peppers and pulse again until a coarse puree results. (If you do not have a food processor or blender, simply chop the onions, green chilies, and jalapeño peppers finely by hand.)

3. Heat butter over medium heat in medium saucepan. When butter sizzles, add chile mixture and salt. Cook 5 minutes, stirring often with a wooden spoon, watching mixture carefully to be sure that it does not burn. When excess moisture has evaporated, remove from heat and stir in warmed half-and-half. Transfer sauce to serving bowl.

4. *Grill monkfish:* Remove monkfish from marinade and arrange fillets on prepared grill. Cook 6 to 8 minutes on each side or until fish has lost its translucent appearance. Transfer to serving platter.

5. Serve immediately with green chile sauce. Pass heated French bread at the table.

Yield: 4 servings (with 1¾ cups sauce)

ORIENTAL KABOBS WITH POOR MAN'S LOBSTER

MARINADE

½ cup rice vinegar
2 cloves garlic, minced
1 teaspoon chopped peeled fresh gingerroot
2 tablespoons soy sauce
¾ teaspoon five spice powder (see note below)

SEAFOOD

1 pound monkfish, cut into 1½-inch chunks
2 oranges, cut into quarters
½ cup snow peas, outer string removed, trimmed
1 6½-ounce can water chestnuts, drained
4 10- to 12-inch wooden skewers, soaked in water 30 minutes and drained
Oil for greasing grill

1. *Prepare marinade:* Combine marinade ingredients in shallow glass bowl or pie plate.
2. Arrange fish in marinade and marinate for 1 hour, turning after 30 minutes. Drain monkfish, reserving marinade.
3. Thread orange quarters, snow peas, water chestnuts, and monkfish on skewers. Brush with marinade.
4. *Grill monkfish:* Arrange skewers on greased grill over ashen coals, about 3 to 4 inches from heat source. Cook 4 to 5 minutes on each side or until lightly browned. Turn skewers as necessary and brush with marinade. Serve immediately with hot brown rice or Oriental noodles.
Note: Five spice powder is available at Oriental food stores and in the Oriental food sections of some supermarkets.

Yield: 4 servings

POOR MAN'S LOBSTER WITH CONCARNEU SAUCE

We had some leftover grilled monkfish and ate it the following day, served cold and sliced with warm sauce. It tasted even more like lobster, firm and somewhat sweet in taste. Concarneu sauce hails from Brittany's rocky coast.

CONCARNEU SAUCE
2 tablespoons butter
1 tablespoon olive oil
1 small onion, minced
3 medium shallots, minced
1 clove garlic, minced
1 tablespoon all-purpose flour
4 medium-large tomatoes, peeled, seeded, and chopped
1 tablespoon tomato paste
3 tablespoons minced fresh parsley
2 teaspoons minced fresh tarragon
¾ cup dry white wine
¼ teaspoon salt
⅛ teaspoon freshly ground pepper

MARINADE
6 tablespoons salad oil
2 tablespoons lemon juice
1 clove garlic, minced
¼ teaspoon salt
⅛ teaspoon freshly ground pepper

SEAFOOD
3 pounds monkfish (sometimes this fish is uneven in thickness; we butterflied the thicker part for more even grilling)

1. *Make Concarneu sauce:* Heat butter and olive oil in a medium saucepan. Sauté onion, shallots, and 1 clove minced garlic over medium heat for 3 to 4 minutes or until tender, stirring often, taking care that it doesn't brown. Whisk in flour and stir until it is absorbed. Add tomatoes, tomato paste, parsley, tarragon, and white wine. Simmer sauce for 10 minutes. Season with salt and pepper; set aside.

2. *Marinate monkfish:* Combine marinade ingredients in a shallow glass bowl or pie plate. Place fish in marinade and marinate for 1 hour, turning after 30 minutes.

3. *Grill monkfish:* Place drained fish on prepared grill and cook for 8 minutes. Brush with remaining marinade and turn. Continue cooking 8 minutes or until fish is cooked. Remember that cooking time depends on the heat of the coals, the distance from the coals, and the thickness of the fish you are preparing. Fish is cooked when it begins to flake when tested with a fork.

4. Place fish on platter, cut into serving pieces, and top with heated sauce.

Yield: 6 servings (with about 2 cups sauce)

MUSSELS

For grilling purposes, we found that it was not necessary to "feed" these bivalve mollusks cornmeal or flour to force them to unload the grit lodged in their shells and intestines. So many of the mussels marketed today are farm grown that they are naturally much cleaner than those marketed just a few years ago. All you'll need to do is wash the shell and pull away any protruding "hairs" (called the *beard*) sticking out of the shell before putting them right on the grill in their shells.

TO CLEAN MUSSELS:

If you cannot find farm-raised mussels, you'll need to clean the mussels.

Tools: wire brush, small sharp knife, bucket, flour or cornmeal.

Scrub the mussel shells with a wire brush, then use a small sharp knife to remove any barnacles. Pull out all seaweed fibers (the beard) sticking out of the shell. Next, put the mussels in a bucket of cold water with a handful of cornmeal or flour. After a while, the mussels will begin to gurgle and bubble. Let them sit in this water one to two hours. Remove them from the pot and rinse them under cold running tap water. If you skip this step after you've allowed them to soak, the mussels will feel slick to the touch. Then pull out any additional fibers that may be sticking out of the shell.

TO OPEN MUSSELS BEFORE GRILLING:

Simply steam them above simmering water, broth, or court bouillon for 3 minutes. Discard any unopened mussels.

GRILLED MUSSELS ON THE HALF SHELL

GARLIC/BACON BREADING

4 tablespoons butter
2 cloves garlic, minced
4 strips bacon, cooked, drained, and crumbled
1¼ cups fine bread crumbs
¼ teaspoon salt
⅛ teaspoon freshly ground pepper

SHELLFISH

2 dozen black mussels, cleaned

1. *Steam mussels:* Put ½ inch water in large kettle, add mussels, cover pot, bring to a boil, and steam 2–3 minutes. Drain mussels, remove top half of shells, and cool. Discard any unopened mussels.

2. *Prepare garlic/bacon breading:* Heat butter in a heavy frying pan; sauté garlic in it until soft, about 1 minute. Stir in bacon bits, bread crumbs, salt, and pepper. Toss to combine; remove from heat and set aside.

3. *Prepare shellfish:* Lightly top each mussel with 2 teaspoons of garlic breading.

4. *Grill mussels:* Place mussels open side up on grill over hot coals. Cover and grill for 3 to 4 minutes. Test one mussel and continue grilling until cooked to taste. Serve hot.

Yield: 4 appetizer servings

MUSSELS ON THE COALS

Aluminum foil
2 dozen small mussels, cleaned
1 7-ounce can baby corn ears, drained
4 green onions, chopped
8 broccoli pieces
4 tablespoons (½ stick) butter
4 tablespoons white wine

1. *Prepare mussel packages:* Cut 4 double sheets of aluminum foil large enough to hold mussels and vegetables.

2. Arrange mussels, corn, and green onions in center of each foil sheet. Add broccoli, dot with butter, and sprinkle with wine.

3. *Grill mussels:* Secure packages tightly. Place directly on hot coals. Cook for 3 to 4 minutes, turn packages, and grill 2 to 3 minutes longer. Test one package to see if it is done. Discard any unopened mussels. Serve hot.

Yield: 4 appetizer servings

MUSSELS WITH MARINARA SAUCE

MARINARA SAUCE

¼ cup good-quality olive oil
2 cloves garlic, minced
½ cup chopped green onion
1 28-ounce can tomatoes chopped, with liquid
¼ teaspoon dried thyme
1 bay leaf
¼ cup dry white wine
3 tablespoons minced Italian parsley
Salt and pepper to taste

SHELLFISH

3 to 4 4-inch pieces mesquite *or* 2 cups mesquite chips,
   soaked in water 1 hour and drained
2½ dozen medium-sized mussels, cleaned

1. *Prepare marinara sauce:* Heat oil in a small heavy saucepan.
Sauté garlic and onion in it until lightly browned. Stir in tomatoes with
their liquid. Add thyme, bay leaf, wine, parsley, salt, and pepper. Cook
over medium heat for 15 minutes, stirring occasionally.

2. *Grill mussels:* Arrange mesquite wood over hot coals and
carefully replace grill. Arrange mussels over grill in the center. Cover
and smoke for 3 to 5 minutes or until done. Discard any unopened
mussels. Divide mussels among wide soup plates. Ladle hot sauce over
mussels.

Yield: 4 servings

65

MUSSEL-CLAM KABOBS

DRESSING

1   cup tarragon vinegar
½   cup good-quality olive oil
1   tablespoon chopped fresh parsley
1   clove garlic, minced
½   teaspoon paprika

SHELLFISH

1   dozen medium clams, shucked
1   dozen mussels, cleaned and shucked
8   broccoli flowerets
12 cherry tomatoes
1   large red onion, quartered and leaves separated
4   10-inch wooden skewers, soaked in water 30 minutes
and drained
Oil for greasing grill

1. *Prepare dressing:* Pour vinegar into a bowl and whisk in olive oil, parsley, garlic, and paprika. Set aside.

2. Divide shellfish and vegetables and thread on skewers. Brush generously with dressing.

3. *Grill kabobs:* Arrange kabobs on prepared grill over ashen coals and grill for 2 to 3 minutes. Brush with dressing and continue grilling for 2 to 3 minutes or until done. Serve hot.

Yield: 4 servings

HICKORY-SMOKED MUSSELS
WITH FRUIT COMPOTE

These smoked mussels can also be shelled after grilling and tossed in a green salad or pasta salad.

SUMMER FRUIT COMPOTE

¼   cup water
½   cup sugar
½   teaspoon ground cinnamon
½   teaspoon ground ginger
6   peaches, peeled (see note below) and sliced
1   pint raspberries, washed and drained
2   cups seedless red grapes, washed and drained
4   cooking apples or other fruit of your choice, peeled, cored, and sliced

SHELLFISH

3   cups hickory chips, soaked in water 30 minutes and drained
3   dozen mussels, cleaned

1. *Prepare fruit compote:* Bring water and sugar to boil in medium pan. Reduce heat to simmer, add spices and fruit, and stir to combine. Continue simmering for 5 minutes, stirring occasionally. Cool, pour fruit into bowl, and refrigerate until ready to serve.

2. *Smoke mussels:* Sprinkle drained hickory chips over hot coals and carefully replace grill. Arrange mussels in center of grill. Cover and smoke for 6 minutes or until done. Discard any unopened mussels. Mussels can be served warm or hot with the fruit compote.

Note: To remove the skin of the peaches soak the peaches in boiling water 2 minutes, then rinse with cold water. The skins can then be removed easily.

Yield: 6 appetizer servings

MUSSELS STUFFED WITH SHRIMP PASTE

SHRIMP PASTE

4   medium shallots, minced
2   cloves garlic, minced
½   pound small shrimp, cooked, shelled, and pureed
1   egg, slightly beaten
¼   teaspoon salt
⅛   teaspoon white pepper

SHELLFISH

2   dozen mussels, cleaned

1. *Prepare shrimp paste:* Combine shrimp paste ingredients in a small bowl. Set aside.

2. *Steam mussels:* Put ½ inch water in a medium pot. Bring to a boil. Put in mussels, cover, and steam about 2 to 3 minutes. Discard any mussels that do not open. Cool. Discard top shells. Lightly top each mussel with 1 teaspoon of shrimp paste.

3. *Grill mussels:* Arrange mussels on grill over ashen coals. Cover and grill for 3 to 4 minutes or until done. Serve hot.

Yield: 4 appetizer servings

MUSSELS WITH BLACK BEAN SAUCE

For a slightly different flavor, try adding 3 cups mesquite chips or hickory chips, soaked in water for 30 minutes and drained, over the hot coals.

BLACK BEAN SAUCE

2 tablespoons dry white wine
½ teaspoon sugar
2 tablespoons soy sauce
6 tablespoons chicken stock
1½ teaspoons cornstarch blended with 2 tablespoons water
2 tablespoons peanut oil
2 tablespoons salted black beans (available at Oriental food stores), washed, drained, and mashed with back of spoon
3 cloves garlic, minced
½ teaspoon minced peeled fresh gingerroot
½ teaspoon crushed red pepper
2 green onions, minced
2 red bell peppers, seeded and cut into ¾-inch strips

SHELLFISH

2 dozen medium-sized farm-grown mussels, cleaned
Oil for greasing grill

1. *Prepare black bean sauce:* Combine wine, sugar, soy sauce, and stock. Whisk in cornstarch mixture. Set aside.
2. Heat oil in wok or heavy skillet. Add black beans, garlic, ginger, crushed red pepper, and green onions. Cook for 1 minute on high heat, stirring continuously. Add pepper and wine mixture and stir until sauce thickens slightly, about 2 minutes. Set aside.
3. *Grill mussels:* Arrange mussels on prepared grill. Cover and cook for 5 minutes. Discard any unopened mussels.
4. Place mussels in a deep heavy bowl. Drizzle hot black bean sauce over mussels. Serve immediately.

Yield: 4 appetizer servings

SKEWERED GREEN LIP MUSSELS, SHRIMP, AND KIWIFRUIT WITH KIWIFRUIT BEURRE BLANC SAUCE

Green lip mussels are large, tender, meaty mussels from New Zealand, yielding about eight to a pound. They are available fresh in the shell at the fishmarket or frozen and packaged at Oriental food markets.

KIWIFRUIT BEURRE BLANC SAUCE
2   kiwifruit, peeled
4   medium shallots, minced
1   cup dry white wine
½   pound (2 sticks) butter, cut into ½-inch pieces

SHELLFISH
½   cup water
½   cup dry white wine
2   large bay leaves
1   small carrot, sliced thin
1   pound green lip mussels, cleaned
¾   pound large shrimp, shelled and deveined
8   cherry tomatoes
2   kiwifruit, cut into quarters (unpeeled)
4   green onions, cut into 2-inch pieces
4   10-inch wooden skewers, soaked in water 30 minutes and drained
Melted butter for brushing kabobs
Oil for greasing grill
Kiwifruit slices (for garnish)

    1. *Prepare sauce:* Puree 1 peeled kiwifruit and reserve. Slice the other peeled kiwifruit and set aside for garnish. Combine shallots, 1 cup wine, and kiwifruit puree in heavy nonaluminum saucepan; reduce mixture to 2 to 3 tablespoons. Remove saucepan from heat, add 1 piece of butter, and whisk until incorporated. Whisk in remaining butter, 2 pieces at a time, being careful not to allow the sauce to separate. If

sauce separates, whisk quickly and try to emulsify. Keep sauce warm over simmering water or serve immediately.

2. *Steam mussels:* Combine water, $\frac{1}{2}$ cup wine, bay leaves, and carrot in a medium saucepan. Bring mixture to a boil over medium-high heat. Add mussels, cover, and steam for 2 to 3 minutes, shaking pan during cooking. Discard any unopened mussels. Remove mussels from shells and set aside to cool.

3. Thread mussels, shrimp, tomatoes, quartered kiwifruit, and onions on skewers, beginning with and ending with shrimp. Mussels are threaded horizontally onto skewers. Brush with melted butter.

4. *Grill kabobs:* Arrange skewers on greased grill over ashen coals, about 3 to 4 inches from heat source. Cook 3 to 4 minutes on each side or until lightly browned. Tend to undercook shrimp and barely grill mussels. Serve immediately on bed of rice on individual plates. Garnish with kiwifruit slices. Drizzle with sauce.

Yield: 4 servings

OYSTERS

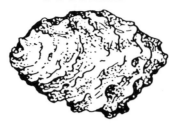

In this chapter, three recipes call for grilling the oysters in the shell; the fourth calls for shucking them first.

TO SHUCK OYSTERS:

Tool: oyster knife (a narrow, short, thick-bladed knife in a wooden handle).

After you wash the oyster shell under running water, locate the weakest point in the shell. To do this, look hard at the flat shell, which is the top one. You will see rings—similar to a spiral—which are formed as the oyster grows. Study the spiral for a moment to locate the place where the rings stopped growing. This will be opposite and a little to the left of the hinge. This is the weakest part of the oyster shell.

As soon as you've found it, lay the oyster on a pot holder with the hinge facing to the left. Grab the oyster and pot holder together securely; your fingers will be under the pot holder, and your thumb should be touching the top of the oyster shell to hold it securely. Insert the point of your oyster knife at the weakest point in the shell. Pry the shell open. It will be a little hard to open, but it can be done. If the shell opens too easily, without any resistance, discard the oyster. Difficulty in opening it means the muscle is still functioning. Run the oyster knife around the shell to loosen the muscle from the hinge. Then remove oysters and use as directed.

You might also want to open fresh oysters, remove them from their shells, and skewer them for grilling. To do this, you'll need to protect the oysters by breading them lightly before grilling.

OYSTER ROAST ON THE GRILL

Oysters can be cooked very successfully in the shell on the grill—a welcome change from struggling to open them by hand. But, whatever kind of oysters you use, be sure to lay a bed of leaves, parsley, lemon slices, or seaweed on the grill first, to act as protection, then place oysters on this in a single layer.

Gremolata is an Italian seasoning mix made most often of chopped garlic, parsley, and finely chopped lemon rind, although other ingredients are sometimes used. The gremolata is then passed around the table to garnish soups and stews. Some cooks sprinkle gremolata directly on the grilled oysters, but we've made the gremolata into a butter, which adds both richness and moisture to the grilled oysters. Six oysters, as we call for here, are an appetizer serving. To make a main dish, serve at least 12 each.

GREMOLATA BUTTER

½ pound (2 sticks) unsalted butter, very soft but not melted
⅓ cup chopped fresh parsley
1 teaspoon finely minced garlic
1 teaspoon finely minced shallots
1 teaspoon finely grated lemon

SHELLFISH

24 oysters in the shell

1. *Prepare gremolata butter:* Mix butter, parsley, garlic, shallots, and lemon rind together well. Transfer to four small bowls (French stoneware butter containers work well) and place on the serving table. (If you make gremolata butter early in the day, cover it carefully before storing in the refrigerator so it doesn't perfume everything else; remember to remove it from the refrigerator 2 hours in advance of serving so it softens sufficiently.)

2. *Grill oysters:* Scrub oysters with a vegetable brush under running tap water and place in shells on grill in a single layer. Grill oysters just a few moments, until you hear little popping noises, which signals that their shells have opened. Serve immediately, using tongs to transfer oysters to serving platter. Spoon soft gremolata butter onto each oyster.

Yield: 4 appetizer servings

GRILLED OYSTERS WITH COGNAC BUTTER

COGNAC BUTTER

½ pound (2 sticks) butter, at room temperature
6   tablespoons chopped pecans
2   teaspoons orange rind
1   tablespoon cognac or to taste

SHELLFISH

24 oysters in the shell

1. *Prepare butter:* Place butter, pecans, orange rind, and cognac in food processor container or blender and process with steel blade until combined. Taste and adjust seasonings, adding more cognac or orange rind as desired. Transfer to serving dish, cover, and refrigerate. Bring to room temperature before serving.

2. *Prepare and grill oysters:* Scrub oysters with a vegetable brush under running tap water and place in shells on grill in single layer. Grill oysters just a few moments, anywhere from about 3 to 6 minutes, depending on size of oysters and grill and/or outdoor temperature. Cover grill. You will hear little popping sounds as each oyster opens. Using tongs, transfer oysters to serving platter carefully, so liquid does not spill. Spoon softened cognac butter onto each oyster.

Yield: 6 servings

GRILLED OYSTERS WITH CAPER BUTTER

CAPER BUTTER
½   pound (2 sticks) butter, at room temperature
2   tablespoons capers, drained
Small bunch fresh parsley, stems removed
1   teaspoon tarragon

SHELLFISH
24 oysters in the shell

    1. *Prepare butter:* Place butter, capers, parsley, and tarragon in food processor container or blender and process with steel blade until well combined. Transfer to serving bowl, cover, and refrigerate. Let butter come to room temperature before serving.

    2. *Prepare and grill oysters:* Scrub oysters with a vegetable brush under running tap water and place in shells on grill in single layer. Grill oysters just 3 to 6 minutes or until you hear little popping noises which indicate the oysters have opened. Serve immediately, using tongs to transfer oysters to serving platter and taking care that liquid does not spill. Serve topped with caper butter.

Yield: 6 servings

AUSTRALIAN CARPETBAG STEAK

This dish comes as close to being the Australian national dish as any. It consists of good-quality beefsteak that is filled with absolutely fresh oysters. If you decide to make it, either open your own oysters immediately before stuffing the steak or make arrangements with your fishmonger to open them just a few minutes before you pick them up. For directions on opening oysters, see Index.

We have added a marinade for the steak based on the Australian lager called Foster, which we think greatly improves the dish. Carpetbag steak is traditionally made by cutting a pocket in the steak, rather than butterflying it. In our version, we butterfly the steak since this exposes more meat surfaces to the marinade.

1 2½- to 3-pound piece boneless sirloin (top butt), all fat removed, about 3 inches thick

MARINADE

1½ cups Foster beer (Australian lager)
½ cup salad oil
4 cloves garlic, minced fine
3 tablespoons fresh lemon juice
¼ cup brown sugar
1 teaspoon salt
1 teaspoon dry mustard
½ teaspoon freshly ground pepper
⅛ teaspoon Tabasco sauce

SHELLFISH

8–12 plump ultrafresh shucked oysters
Tabasco sauce for sprinkling on oysters
Oil for greasing grill

1. Butterfly sirloin steak, splitting it lengthwise so that it opens like a book.

2. *Prepare marinade:* Combine marinade ingredients in a bowl. Place sirloin in plastic bag, pour marinade over top, and secure bag with twister seal. Turn bag several times to make sure that all surfaces of meat touch marinade. Place bag in bowl and let marinate at room temperature for 2 hours.

3. Remove steak from marinade and open "book." Fill inside with oysters, shaking a drop of Tabasco sauce on each oyster. Close book edges together with round wooden toothpicks, poultry skewers, or barbecue skewers.

4. *Grill steak:* Place sirloin on well-oiled, heated barbecue grill and cook about 8 to 10 minutes on each side, depending on degree of doneness desired.

Yield: 4 large servings

SCALLOPS

These bivalve mollusks are usually shelled by the time they come to market, whether they are bay (tiny) scallops or sea (large, marshmallow-size) scallops. If you do find some in the shell, you can put them on the grill to open, but since their shells are thin, set them on a layer of seaweed or leaves or put some other protective material on the grill. If you cannot get scallops fresh, the frozen are quite acceptable—even more so if they are marinated in our Basic Marinade (see Index).

Tiny bay scallops are sweeter and more delicious than are the larger sea scallops, but the larger ones are more fun to eat. In this chapter we include a skewered combination of bay and sea scallops that is guaranteed to delight your guests.

Whatever size you choose, remember that scallops are delicate and should be served only with delicate sauces and butters. Scallops also take well to marinades.

MARINATED SEA SCALLOPS WITH CLASSIC DRAWN BUTTER

Drawn or clarified butter is butter that has been separated into pure fat and milk solids. The separation occurs naturally if the butter is melted very slowly. Once the butter is melted, three distinct layers form: a top layer of foam, a large middle layer of clear fat and a thin, bottom layer of milk solids. The foam is usually removed with a spoon and the resultant clear fat poured into a clean bowl, leaving the milky solids in the bottom of the melting pan to be discarded. The method used here— making individual drawn butter portions by putting quarter-pound butter sticks into narrow glasses—is used by many restaurants.

2 pounds sea scallops
1 recipe Basic Marinade (see Index)
4 sticks (1 pound) unsalted butter
Oil for greasing grill
2 lemons, quartered
Parsley or watercress sprigs for garnish (optional)

1. *Marinate scallops:* Place sea scallops in a plastic bag and pour marinade over top. Close bag with twister seal and set in a bowl at room temperature for 1 hour. Turn bag a few times as scallops marinate, taking care that all surfaces of scallops are exposed to the marinade.

2. *Clarify butter:* Boil water in a high-sided baking pan, making sure the water won't flow over the top of the glasses you choose. Place four small, narrow glasses in boiling water, then place 1 stick unsalted butter in each. Turn off the heat and allow 20 to 30 minutes to melt. Let glasses remain in hot water until ready to serve.

3. *Grill scallops:* Remove scallops from marinade and arrange them in a single layer in a grill basket or place them on the prepared grill. Cook for 2 to 3 minutes on each side or until scallops have lost their translucent appearance.

4. While scallops grill, spoon off foam from the top of each glass with a spoon, then bring the glasses to the table. Serve scallops immediately, dividing them among guests. Garnish each serving with lemon wedges and a few sprigs of parsley or watercress if desired. Guests will be able to dip scallops in the butter or pour it over them at the table. Explain that the solids should be left undisturbed at the bottom of the glass. Each quarter-pound stick of butter melted this way will result in 5 to 6 tablespoons of pure clarified butter.

Yield: 4 servings

SKEWERED BAY AND SEA SCALLOPS WITH HONEY BUTTER

SHELLFISH

2   pounds sea scallops (about 48 large scallops)

½   pound bay scallops (about 32 small scallops)

6   10-inch wooden skewers, soaked in water 30 minutes and drained

1   recipe Basic Marinade (see Index)

Oil for greasing grill

HONEY BUTTER

4   tablespoons honey

10 tablespoons melted butter

1   tablespoon fresh lemon juice

2   tablespoons white wine

1. Arrange sea and bay scallops on skewers in alternating fashion as follows: two big scallops, three small scallops, two big scallops, three small scallops, etc. Use big scallops at ends of skewers.

2. *Marinate scallops:* Place skewers on a flat pan with raised sides and pour marinade over top. Let sit for 1 hour at room temperature, basting skewers and turning them in marinade often.

3. *Prepare honey butter:* Mix honey, melted butter, lemon juice, and wine together.

4. *Grill scallops:* Remove skewers from marinade and place on prepared grill. Cook about 4 minutes or just until scallops have lost their opaque look, turning skewers once if desired. Serve immediately, passing honey butter to spoon over scallops.

Yield: 6 servings

CURRIED MARINATED SEA SCALLOPS

SHELLFISH
2   pounds sea scallops
Oil for greasing grill

MARINADE
1   cup plain yogurt
1   medium onion
6   cloves garlic
¼   cup sugar
2   tablespoons curry powder (Madras, if possible)
2   tablespoons fresh lemon juice
1   teaspoon cayenne pepper
1   teaspoon salt

GARNISH
Commercial sweetened flaked coconut
1   small jar (approximately 6 ounces) chutney

1. *Marinate scallops:* Place scallops in plastic bag and set bag in bowl. Combine marinade ingredients in food processor container. Process until a coarse puree results. Pour marinade into plastic bag and secure with twister seal. Turn bag several times, making sure all scallop surfaces touch marinade. Let sit at room temperature 2 hours or refrigerate 4 hours, turning occasionally.
2. *Grill scallops:* At serving time, remove scallops from marinade. Place scallops on prepared grill and cook 2 to 3 minutes on each side, watching carefully. Transfer to serving platter and serve immediately. Pass bowls of coconut and chutney for sprinkling.

Yield: 4 servings

SEA SCALLOPS IN AN ALMOND CRUST

3   eggs
2   tablespoons snipped fresh chives
½   teaspoon salt
¼   teaspoon cayenne pepper
8   ounces blanched almonds, chopped fine or ground into powder
2   pounds sea scallops
¼   cup sliced almonds
½   cup butter
Oil for greasing grill

1. Mix eggs, chives, salt, and cayenne in a small bowl. Sprinkle ground almonds into a large, flat platter in as thin a layer as possible.

2. Dry scallops on paper towels. Dip scallops into egg mixture, then roll them in ground almonds. Arrange coated scallops in a single layer on a plate and refrigerate for at least 30 minutes.

3. Meanwhile, sprinkle ¼ cup sliced almonds in a single layer on a baking sheet and place in a 350°F oven for about 6 to 8 minutes or until almonds are just beginning to turn golden. Remove from oven immediately and let cool.

4. Melt butter in a small saucepan. Stir in toasted almond slices. Let sit until ready to serve.

5. *Grill scallops:* Arrange scallops carefully on a well-oiled grill. Cook 2 to 3 minutes on each side, turning carefully. Scallops must be watched so the almond coating does not burn.

6. Transfer scallops to serving platter. Spoon melted butter and toasted almond slices into sauceboat. Serve immediately, passing melted butter-almond sauce.

Yield: 4 servings

SCALLOP ANTIPASTO KABOBS

The following grilled antipasto works beautifully as a main course or as an appetizer. To serve as an entree, double the ingredients, serving 2 skewers each.

4   skewers
1   2-ounce chunk prosciutto cut into 4 skewer-size pieces
4   scallions, white parts only, each cut into 3 lengths
24 sea scallops
4   jarred pepperoncini
4   large pitted black olives
4   canned artichoke hearts, well drained
4   small, firm Italian tomatoes
1   2-ounce piece Genoa salami or cappicola, cut into 4
    skewer-size pieces
½   cup extra-virgin olive oil
2   large cloves garlic, chopped fine
Oil for greasing grill

1. *Marinate kabobs:* Thread all ingredients except oil and garlic onto four skewers in alternating fashion. Lay skewers on platter. Mix olive oil and garlic and brush skewered ingredients liberally with mixture, making sure that canned artichoke hearts get a liberal dose of oil/garlic mixture inside. Let sit at room temperature for 20 minutes, brushing with mixture occasionally.

2. *Grill kabobs:* Lay skewers on prepared grill. Grill 3 to 4 minutes on each side, until scallops are done and remaining ingredients are charred on the edges. Serve with heated Italian bread.

Yield: 4 servings

SCALLOPS ON A BED OF SPINACH

SPINACH

1   10-ounce package frozen spinach, chopped fine
3   ounces shallots, chopped fine
1   cup dry white wine
1   tablespoon butter
1   tablespoon flour
1   cup half-and-half
½   teaspoon salt
¼   teaspoon grated nutmeg

SHELLFISH

2   pounds sea scallops
4   10-inch wooden skewers, soaked in water 30 minutes
    and drained
Vegetable oil for brushing scallops

1. Cook spinach according to package directions, then transfer to strainer. Press spinach with the back of a wooden spoon until most of the moisture has been extracted. Spinach should measure 1 scant cup.

2. Meanwhile, place shallots and wine in a small saucepan and simmer until both wine and shallots measure scant ½ cup.

3. Melt butter in a medium saucepan, then add flour and cook for a moment, stirring constantly with a wire whisk, until butter/flour mixture bubbles and is golden. Slowly add half-and-half, stirring constantly with whisk. Continue cooking, whisking frequently, until mixture is smooth and thickened and coats a spoon.

4. Add shallot/wine mixture and spinach to cream sauce. Stir to combine, then add salt and nutmeg. Continue cooking for about 5 minutes.

5. *Grill scallops:* Meanwhile, skewer scallops loosely, then brush with oil on both sides. Place skewers on a heated, well-oiled grill and cook 2 to 3 minutes on each side, or as long as necessary until scallops are cooked through and have lost their translucency.

6. Transfer hot spinach to a large serving platter with slightly raised sides. Unskewer scallops carefully onto spinach, arranging them in an attractive fashion. Serve immediately.

Yield: 4 servings

SEA SCALLOPS WRAPPED IN BACON AND GOAT CHEESE

You will need 2 teaspoons goat cheese and a ½ slice of bacon for each scallop in the following dish. If desired, substitute cream cheese or mix equal parts of Roquefort and cream cheese to stuff bacon. Soft feta cheese and chive cream cheese are also good substitutes for goat cheese, although the feta and bacon together are somewhat salty. Half-cooked bacon pieces are also delicious wrapped around shrimp.

16 slices bacon
1½–2 cups mild goat cheese, such as Montrachet
32 large sea scallops
Round wooden toothpicks
Oil for greasing grill

1. *Cook bacon:* Place bacon in large frying pan and sauté over low heat 4 to 5 minutes or until half cooked. Drain bacon on paper towels, pressing on all sides to absorb fat. Cut bacon slices in half to yield 32 pieces.
2. *Wrap scallops:* Spread each bacon piece with 2 teaspoons goat cheese. Wrap one piece of bacon with goat cheese around each scallop, using toothpick to secure. Continue wrapping bacon and goat cheese around scallops until all are prepared.
3. *Grill scallops:* Place bacon-wrapped scallops in a single layer on an oiled grill and cook 2 to 3 minutes or until bacon is cooked. Turn and cook on remaining side if necessary. Serve immediately.

Yield: 4 servings

SCALLOPS IN SZECHWAN SAUCE

SHELLFISH

2   pounds sea scallops
1   recipe Basic Marinade (see Index)
8   10-inch wooden skewers, soaked in water 30 minutes
    and drained
Oil for greasing grill

SZECHWAN SAUCE

1   1-inch piece fresh gingerroot, peeled and quartered
4   large garlic cloves, quartered
2   green onions, cut into pieces
2   tablespoons vegetable oil
½   teaspoon crushed red pepper
3   tablespoons sugar
5   teaspoons Japanese soy sauce
3   tablespoons catsup
2   tablespoons dry white wine
1   teaspoon white vinegar
1   teaspoon Oriental sesame oil

1. *Marinate scallops:* Place scallops in large plastic bag set in bowl. Pour marinade over. Secure with twister seal and turn to make sure that all surfaces of scallops touch marinade. Let sit at room temperature 1 hour, turning occasionally.

2. Fifteen minutes before scallops are ready to be cooked, combine ginger, garlic, and green onion pieces in food processor container and coarsely chop.

3. Thread drained scallops on skewers.

4. *Prepare sauce:* Heat vegetable oil in heavy-bottomed skillet or wok. Then sauté chopped ginger, garlic, and green onion for about 1 minute.

5. Meanwhile combine red pepper, sugar, soy sauce, catsup, wine, vinegar, and sesame oil. Stir this into onion mixture. Simmer 1 more minute.

6. *Grill scallops*: Place scallops on prepared grill and cook about 2 to 3 minutes on each side or until scallops have lost their translucency.

Remove from heat and transfer to serving platter. Serve guests 2 skewers each and drizzle a few spoonfuls of sauce over scallops.

Yield: 4 servings

SEA SCALLOPS WITH ROE, SERVED WITH CREME FRAICHE AND FRESHWATER CAVIAR

CREME FRAICHE
1   cup heavy cream
1½ tablespoons buttermilk

SHELLFISH
1½ pounds sea scallops with roe (it isn't necessary for all
    of the scallops to have the roe)
Melted butter for brushing scallops
Oil for greasing grill basket
12-ounces freshwater caviar (see note below)

1. *Prepare Crème Fraîche:* Prepare the crème fraîche the day before it is needed in recipe. Combine heavy cream and buttermilk in a sterilized jar. Leave jar on kitchen counter in a warm area. Turn jar occasionally. Mixture will thicken in about 12 to 16 hours. Refrigerate until ready to use.

2. *Prepare sea scallops:* Gently wash scallops and pat dry with paper toweling. Brush scallops with melted butter.

3. Arrange in prepared grill basket; close basket. Grill scallops for 3 to 4 minutes over medium-hot heat (coals will be mostly ashen). Turn basket and continue cooking until scallops begin to turn opaque. Remember that scallops, like most fish and shellfish, are best slightly undercooked.

4. Remove scallops and arrange on four plates. Drizzle with crème fraîche and top with caviar. Serve with a light pasta.

Note: The caviar used in this recipe is available from Carolyn Collins Caviar (see Appendix for address).

Yield: 4 servings

SEA SCALLOPS WITH HOMEMADE JALAPEÑO MAYONNAISE

SHELLFISH

2 pounds sea scallops
1 recipe Basic Marinade (see Index)
Oil for greasing grill

JALAPEÑO MAYONNAISE

1 large egg *or* 2 egg yolks, at room temperature
2 tablespoons white vinegar
1 teaspoon dry mustard
¼ cup good-quality olive oil
¼ teaspoon salt
¼ teaspoon white pepper
½ cup vegetable oil
¼ cup good-quality imported sweet-smelling olive oil
1 handful fresh parsley, washed, stems removed
⅓ cup thawed and thoroughly drained frozen chopped spinach
2 green onions, green part only, cut into 1-inch pieces
2 fresh or canned (packed in vinegar) jalapeño peppers, seeded

1. *Marinate scallops:* Place sea scallops in plastic bag and set bag in large bowl. Pour marinade over scallops and close bag with twister seal. Let sit at room temperature 1 hour, turning occasionally to make certain all scallop surfaces come in contact with marinade.

2. *Prepare sauce:* Rinse blender or food processor container and blade with hot water, dry quickly, and replace on motor unit. Place egg or yolks in warmed container, along with vinegar, dry mustard, ¼ cup olive oil, salt, and white pepper. Pulse twice or enough times to combine.

3. Mix ½ cup vegetable oil with ¼ cup olive oil. Turn food processor on and immediately begin pouring oil into mixture in a thin, steady stream. When all oil has been added, turn food processor off.

4. Add parsley, spinach, green onion pieces, and jalapeños to mixture. Carefully pulse a few times until mixture is finely chopped but has not dissolved into the mayonnaise. Green pieces should be very discernible. Transfer to serving bowl and reserve until scallops are cooked.

5. *Grill scallops:* Remove scallops from marinade and arrange in a single layer on prepared grill in wire grill basket with a narrow grid. Grill scallops 2 to 3 minutes on each side or until they've lost their translucent appearance.

6. Transfer scallops to a heated serving platter. Serve immediately with mayonnaise at room temperature. Use mayonnaise as a dip and pass heated French bread.

Yield: 4 servings (with 1½ cups sauce)

SHRIMP

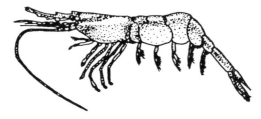

Shrimp are graded according to size and weight by the seafood industry. There are about 30 different grades, which range from the very large (under 5 shrimp per pound) to the very small (72 to 100 per pound). Although large shrimp are sometimes called *prawns*, the American seafood industry frowns on this word, which is descriptive rather than precise.

This crustacean is so popular in this country that shrimp are available everywhere and sold in every possible form: both cooked and raw, both shelled and in the shell. And, of course, you'll find numerous frozen shrimp dishes in the supermarket.

TO SHELL AND CLEAN SHRIMP

Shrimp can be shelled before or after cooking. To shell shrimp, simply tear open the shell on the inside of the curve, where it is the softest, then peel off the remainder. Although it is perfectly safe to eat shrimp without removing the black sand vein located along the curved back (and sometimes along the front) of the shrimp, we prefer the nicety of serving them cleaned. Simply make a shallow cut down the back of the peeled shrimp and wash the black vein out under cold running tap water. If you wish to cook the shrimp in their shells—which protects them on the grill—you may split the shells down the back and remove the vein without removing the shell.

TO SKEWER SHRIMP: THE SERPENTINE METHOD

The serpentine or interlocking method of skewering shrimp is guaranteed to generate comments from your guests. This method can be used when you are grilling plain shrimp or when you want to marinate them beforehand; simply skewer the shrimp in this fashion, then lay them in the marinade, turning occasionally, before grilling. These instructions are based on using medium to large shrimp, shelled and deveined.

Tools: Oriental wooden barbecue skewers (one skewer for every six shrimp).

1. Working with two shrimp at a time, and holding skewer upright, thread the tail of shrimp #1 onto skewer with head curling up on the left side of skewer.

2. Thread tail of shrimp #2 on skewer with head curling up on the right side of skewer.

3. Thread head of shrimp #1 on skewer.

4. Thread head of shrimp #2 on skewer.

5. Push shrimp heads and tails together tightly, then push both interlocked shrimp to the bottom of the skewer.

6. Repeat with next two shrimp; then repeat again with remaining two shrimp. You will end up with three sets of interlocked shrimp. If there is room, arrange an additional set of interlocked shrimp on skewers.

7. Marinate and grill or grill immediately. Serve one or two skewers to each guest, depending on shrimp size.

SESAME-COATED SHRIMP WITH HONEY

4 eggs, well beaten
1½ cups sesame seeds
3 pounds shrimp, shelled and deveined
Oil for greasing grill
1 cup honey

1. Place eggs in bowl and beat well. Pour sesame seeds into a large heavy-bottomed frying pan and place over medium heat. Let seeds heat slightly, then watch carefully, stirring with wooden spoon until seeds start to take on a light brown color (you will smell this before you see it). Pour seeds into large, flat dish and allow to cool sufficiently to handle.

2. Dry shrimp well with paper towels. Dip shrimp in beaten egg, then in sesame seeds. Arrange sesame-coated shrimp on a large platter in a single layer and refrigerate for at least 30 minutes.

3. Place shrimp on hot, well-oiled grill and cook about 3 minutes on each side or until shrimp have lost their translucent appearance. Transfer to serving platter and serve immediately, passing honey. Guests should spoon only a thin stream of honey over sesame shrimp.

Yield: 4 servings

MARINATED SHRIMP WITH FIVE-MINUTE TUNA DUNK

The following dip is made from ingredients that can be kept in the cupboard for use as a fast, last-minute sauce.

SHELLFISH

3   pounds shrimp, shelled and deveined
1   recipe Basic Marinade (see Index)
Oil for greasing grill

SAUCE

2   cloves garlic, peeled and quartered
3   tablespoons red wine vinegar
1   6½-ounce can white albacore tuna, drained
4   anchovy fillets
½   teaspoon drained capers
10 tablespoons good-quality olive oil
¼   cup water
2   tablespoons drained capers (or more if desired) for sprinkling on top of dip and serving at table

1. Place cleaned shrimp in plastic bag and set plastic bag in bowl. Pour marinade into plastic bag over shrimp and use a twister seal to close bag. Turn bag several times, making certain that all sides of shrimp touch marinade. Let sit at room temperature for 1 hour, turning occasionally.

2. *Prepare sauce:* Place garlic, vinegar, tuna, anchovies, ½ teaspoon capers, olive oil, and water in food processor container. Process until mixture is creamy. Transfer to serving bowl. Sprinkle with 2 tablespoons capers or use more if desired. Let sit until ready to serve.

3. *Grill shrimp:* Remove shrimp from marinade and arrange in a single layer on prepared grill. Cook 2 to 3 minutes on each side or until shrimp has lost its translucent appearance. Remove from heat and transfer to large serving platter. Serve immediately with tuna sauce as dip. Pass additional capers at table if desired. Serve with heated French bread.

Yield: 4 servings (with 1½ cups tuna sauce)

SHRIMP IN A GARLIC MARINADE

SHELLFISH
3 pounds shrimp, shelled and deveined

MARINADE
1 cup imported good-quality mild olive oil
6 tablespoons fresh lemon juice
½ small onion, quartered
4 large cloves garlic, quartered
½ teaspoon salt
½ teaspoon freshly ground pepper

DRAWN BUTTER
4 sticks (1 pound) unsalted butter
4 garlic cloves, peeled and mashed (optional)

1. Place plastic bag in large bowl and fill bag with shrimp.
2. *Prepare marinade:* Place marinade ingredients in food processor container. Process until combined and onion and garlic are chopped fine. Pour into plastic bag over shrimp and secure with twister seal. Turn bag a few times, making sure that all surfaces of shrimp touch marinade. Let sit at room temperature for 1 hour, turning occasionally.
3. *Prepare drawn butter:* Follow directions in recipe for Marinated Sea Scallops with Classic Drawn Butter (see Index). If desired, add a peeled, mashed garlic clove to each drawn butter serving as soon as it has been skimmed of the top foam. Remove garlic before serving.
4. Arrange drained shrimp in a single layer in a wire grill basket. Grill 3 to 4 minutes on each side or until shrimp appears cooked. Transfer to serving platter. Serve with drawn butter.

Yield: 4 servings

SHRIMP GRILLED ON A BED OF TARRAGON

This dish is best prepared in the fall, when herbs are plentiful.

MARINADE

½ cup good-quality olive oil
3 tablespoons fresh lime juice
1 bay leaf
1 clove garlic, minced

SHELLFISH

1½ pounds medium-large shrimp (21–25 per pound),
    peeled, deveined, and washed
Oil for greasing grill
3 cups fresh tarragon
½ teaspoon fennel seeds

1. *Marinate shrimp:* Combine olive oil, lime juice, bay leaf, and garlic in a shallow glass bowl or pie plate. Pat shrimp dry, arrange in marinade, and marinate for 1 hour, turning after 30 minutes. Drain shrimp.

2. *Grill shrimp:* Arrange a bed of tarragon on prepared grill. Place shrimp on the tarragon. Sprinkle shrimp with fennel. Some of the leaves will fall into the grill on the hot coals, adding their own special essence to the shrimp. Turn shrimp after 2 minutes. Continue grilling for 2 minutes or until shrimp are cooked to taste. Serve shrimp tossed in your favorite pasta salad, plain, or on a salad of Bibb lettuce and yellow cherry tomatoes.

Yield: 4–5 servings

SHRIMP IN A KOREAN-STYLE MARINADE

SHELLFISH
3 pounds shrimp, shelled and deveined

KOREAN MARINADE
⅓ cup Japanese soy sauce
⅓ cup water
⅓ cup Oriental dark sesame oil
2 tablespoons sugar
5 garlic cloves, peeled and halved
1 2-inch-long piece fresh gingerroot, peeled and quartered
2 teaspoons sesame seeds

1. Place shrimp in a large plastic bag and set bag in a large bowl.

2. *Prepare marinade:* Put soy sauce, water, sesame oil, sugar, garlic, and ginger in food processor or blender container and process until garlic and ginger are chopped fine. (If you do not own a food processor, put garlic through press and chop ginger fine by hand).

3. Pour mixture into plastic bag over shrimp and close bag with twister seal. Turn bag a few times so all surfaces of shrimp are exposed to marinade. Let sit at room temperature 30 minutes, turning bag often.

4. Sprinkle sesame seeds in a single layer in a small frying pan and place over medium heat. Watch carefully. In a moment or two, seeds will start to brown (you will smell this as it starts to happen). Stir seeds with a wooden spoon and remove pan from heat. Allow seeds to cool in pan, then transfer to tiny serving bowl.

5. *Grill shrimp:* Arrange drained shrimp in a single layer in a grill basket and fasten top as tightly as possible. Place on hot grill and cook about 3 to 4 minutes on each side or until shrimp have turned red and the meat is no longer translucent.

6. Transfer shrimp from basket to serving platter. Sprinkle toasted sesame seeds over top of shrimp. Serve immediately.

Yield: 4 servings

SHRIMP IN AN INDONESIAN MARINADE

This recipe calls for shrimp paste, and inexpensive Oriental shrimp concentrate that comes in a small jar with a screw top and stores in the refrigerator. Shrimp paste is similar to anchovy paste, except that it is much less strongly flavored. It does add an important quality to the flavor of certain dishes. If you have access to an Indonesian or Oriental market nearby, buy your shrimp paste there. If not, you'll find mail-order sources of shrimp paste in the Appendix.

SHELLFISH
3   pounds shrimp, peeled and deveined

INDONESIAN MARINADE
3   tablespoons fresh lemon juice
6   tablespoons water
1   tablespoon sugar
½   teaspoon salt
3   small fresh hot chilies, peeled, seeded, and quartered
¾   teaspoon shrimp paste
6   cloves garlic, peeled and quartered

1. Place shrimp in plastic bag and set bag in bowl.
2. *Prepare marinade:* Mix marinade ingredients in food processor or blender container. Process until a course paste results. (If you have no food processor, chop everything as fine as possible and shake together in a small jar with a lid.)
3. Pour marinade into plastic bag over shrimp and secure with twister seal. Shake and turn bag until all surfaces of shrimp have come in contact with the marinade. Let sit at room temperature 30 minutes, turning bag occasionally.
4. *Grill shrimp:* Empty plastic bag into bowl and arrange shrimp in a single layer in a grill basket with top. Grill about 5 minutes on one side or until shrimp are no longer translucent and they have a grilled appearance. While shrimp grill, baste at least once with marinade remaining in bottom of bowl. Turn basket and grill 3 to 4 minutes or until other side also has a slightly grilled look. Transfer shrimp from wire basket to large serving plate with raised sides. Serve immediately.

Yield: 4 servings

GRILLED SHRIMP WITH FONDUE

FONDUE
1 pound Swiss cheese
1 clove garlic, minced
¼ teaspoon grated nutmeg
2 tablespoons dry white wine (or to taste)
1 tablespoon kirschwasser
4 fondue forks

SHELLFISH
¼ teaspoon white pepper
¼ cup chopped fresh dill
¼ pound (1 stick) butter, melted
1½ pounds large shrimp, shelled and deveined
Oil for greasing grill

1. *Make fondue:* Grate cheese. Combine cheese, garlic, and nutmeg in top of a double boiler over simmering water or in a fondue pot over heat. Cook, stirring often, until smooth. Stir in white wine and kirschwasser. Keep warm until ready to serve.

2. *Grill shrimp:* Blend pepper and fresh dill with melted butter. Brush shrimp with dill butter and arrange on prepared grill or in a double-hinged grill basket. Grill shrimp for 2 to 3 minutes, brush with reserved butter, turn, and continue cooking 1 to 2 minutes or until done.

3. Arrange shrimp on individual plates at the table with the cheese fondue in the center, within easy reach of guests. Using fondue forks, dip the grilled shrimp into the fondue. Serve with thick slices of crusty French bread.

Yield: 4–5 servings

SHRIMP WITH BAGNA CAUDA

*Bagna cauda is a traditional Italian sauce and ritual in which cold
sliced vegetables are dipped into a hot anchovy sauce. The vegetables
usually served in Italy are cardoons, celery, peppers, fennel, cabbage,
cauliflower, and small Italian tomatoes. The dip is traditionally made of
crushed garlic, anchovies, butter, and olive oil, but local variations
include cream, wine, or truffles. Our version is made with sour cream,
but you can substitute sour half-and-half, if desired. If you wish, serve a
platter of vegetables for dipping along with the shrimp.*

SHELLFISH
3   pounds shrimp, shelled and deveined
1   recipe Basic Marinade (see Index)

SAUCE
4   tablespoons butter
4   tablespoons extra-virgin olive oil
6   large cloves garlic, peeled and smashed
1   2-ounce can flat anchovy fillets, drained and chopped
    very fine
1   cup sour cream at room temperature

1. Place cleaned shrimp in a plastic bag. Pour marinade over
shrimp and secure bag with twister seal. Let sit at room temperature
for 1 hour.
2. *Prepare sauce:* Heat butter, oil, garlic, and anchovies together in
a small saucepan over medium heat until butter is melted and mixture
is just about to simmer.
3. Spoon mixture into blender or food processor container. Add
sour cream. Process until smooth. Keep warm until ready to serve; then
transfer to one large dipping bowl or individual dipping bowls.
4. *Grill shrimp:* Remove shrimp from marinade and arrange on
grill or in a grill basket in a single layer. Grill shrimp 2 to 3 minutes on
each side or until they have lost their translucent quality. Transfer
shrimp to heated serving platter and serve immediately, using warm
bagna cauda as a dip. Pass heated French bread.

Yield: 4 servings (with 1½ cups sauce)

PRAWNS ON THE BARBI

Despite actor Paul Hogan's charming TV advertisement for Australia, Australians do not put shrimp on the barbi. They put prawns on the barbi, which is what large shrimp are called down under. Giant, five-inch prawns—the ones most commonly put on Australian barbis—are called king prawns. *Australian barbecues too, are different from the American-style barbecue pictured in the Hogan ad; in Australia, most barbecues are not grids, but are instead solid plates of metal set over a wood fire. According to Ann Mickelson, Information Assistant at the Australian Consulate General's office in Chicago, "Most Australians would use a dipping sauce with prawns on the barbi. This might be something like sour cream or yogurt flavored with dill and cucumber; or it might be an Indonesian-style dipping sauce—one with hot peppers added to make it hot. Australians are very innovative cooks and not only cook dishes from many different cuisines (particularly the surrounding ones, such as Indonesia and Malaysia), but also tend to use whatever is fresh and in season." Some Aussies forgo the sauce entirely, though, and just marinate the shrimp in honey before putting it on the barbi. Although we included a recipe for Indonesian shrimp with a peanut dipping sauce in our book* Fish on the Grill, *the first of this grilled seafood series, we couldn't resist adding this one, which is hotter and entirely different from the recipe in that book.*

SHELLFISH
3 pounds largest shrimp
Oil for greasing grill

MARINADE
1 cup salad oil
⅓ cup fresh lemon juice
½ teaspoon snipped fresh dill *or* ¼ teaspoon dried dill
½ teaspoon salt
¼ teaspoon freshly ground pepper

HOT INDONESIAN PEANUT DIPPING SAUCE

¾ cup peanut butter

4 cloves garlic, peeled and quartered

3 tablespoons Japanese soy sauce

3 tablespoons fresh lemon juice

1 2-inch piece fresh gingerroot, peeled and quartered

2 teaspoons sugar

1 teaspoon crushed red pepper

1 fresh jalapeño pepper, peeled, seeded, and quartered

6 tablespoons water

1. With a sharp knife, split shrimp shells along the back and remove the dark vein under running water. Do not remove shells. Place shrimp in large plastic bag and set bag in large bowl.

2. *Marinate shrimp:* Combine marinade ingredients in a small bowl. Pour marinade into bag filled with shrimp. Secure with twister seal. Turn bag several times to be sure all surfaces of shrimp touch marinade. Let sit at room temperature for 1 hour.

3. Prepare dipping sauce: Place sauce ingredients in a food processor or blender container and process until coarsely pureed. Transfer to a serving bowl or use four individual dipping bowls.

4. *Grill shrimp:* At serving time, remove shrimp from marinade and place on heated, well-oiled grill. Cook giant shrimp about 4 minutes on each side, watching very carefully so shrimp are removed from grill at exact point of doneness. Transfer to serving platter and serve immediately with dipping sauce.

Yield: 4 servings (with 1½ cups sauce)

GARLIC-STUFFED SHRIMP, THAI STYLE

Three different ethnic cuisines use the commercial bottled fish sauce called for in this recipe. It is known as nam pla *in Thai food stores,* nuoc mam *in Vietnamese food stores and* tuk trey *in Cambodian food stores. Although bottled fish sauce sounds like it would taste and smell just awful, it is actually very mild in scent and flavor and adds substantially to the final taste of the dish.* Nam pla *is available at Vietnamese markets (or see Appendix).*

FILLING

6   tablespoons very finely chopped fresh garlic (chop by hand; do not use a blender or food processor)
1   cup firmly packed fresh bread crumbs (made in blender)
6   teaspoons nam pla (Thailand commercial bottled fish sauce)
1½ teaspoons freshly ground pepper
⅛   teaspoon salt
¼   cup vegetable oil

SHELLFISH

3   pounds large shrimp, shelled, deveined, and butterflied
Oil for brushing shrimp and greasing grill

1. *Prepare filling:* Combine finely chopped garlic, bread crumbs, nam pla, pepper, and salt in a small bowl and mix together well.
2. Heat ¼ cup oil in a small skillet over very low heat and fry mixture very slowly, stirring often with a wooden spoon until it turns golden brown; this should take about 15 minutes.
3. Stuff each shrimp with a small amount of mixture, securing with toothpick, if necessary. Reserve extra filling.
4. *Grill shrimp:* Brush stuffed shrimp with oil lightly on both sides, using a pastry brush, and arrange on prepared grill. Cook shrimp 2 to 3 minutes on each side or until shrimp have lost their translucent appearance and are slightly browned on the edges.
5. Meanwhile, heat remaining filling and transfer to serving bowl. Remove shrimp from grill and transfer to serving platter. Serve immediately, passing bowl of filling to sprinkle over shrimp.

Yield: 4 servings

MARINATED SHRIMP WITH THREE MIDDLE EASTERN DIPS

The combination of three Middle Eastern dips and marinated vegetables makes an interesting Middle Eastern menu.

3 pounds large shrimp, shelled and deveined
1 recipe Basic Marinade (see Index)
Oil for greasing grill
1 recipe each Baba Ghanouj, Tahini Dipping Sauce, and
   Yogurt Cheese Dip (recipes follow)

1. Place shrimp in a plastic bag in a large bowl. Pour basic marinade over shrimp and close bag with twister seal. Turn bag several times, making certain that all sides of shrimp touch marinade. Let sit at room temperature for 1 hour.

2. Make dips (see following recipes) and set out on table in three bowls.

3. *Grill shrimp:* Arrange shrimp in a single layer on prepared grill or in a grill basket. Grill 2 to 3 minutes on each side or until shrimp appear done. Serve immediately with the Middle Eastern dips following this recipe.

Yield: 4 servings

BABA GHANOUJ (EGGPLANT PUREE DIP)

1 medium eggplant, peeled with vegetable peeler and cut
into thin slices
Salt
4 cloves garlic, quartered
2 tablespoons good-quality mild olive oil
¼ cup fresh lemon juice
¼ cup tahini (sesame seed paste; see note below)
1 small handful parsley sprigs, stems removed
Fresh pomegranate seeds for garnish

1. Arrange eggplant slices in a single layer on paper towels and salt
lightly on both sides. Let sit 30 minutes or until enough bitter juices
have run out to discolor towels. Transfer eggplant slices to a foil-covered
baking sheet in a single layer. Bake 20 to 30 minutes at 350°F, until
eggplant has softened and has a cooked appearance.
2. Quarter eggplant slices and put into food processor container.
Add garlic, olive oil, lemon juice, tahini, and parsley sprigs. Process to
combine, making a coarse puree. Transfer to an attractive serving bowl
and sprinkle with pomegranate seeds. (If you have no food processor,
simply chop everything fine and combine.)

Note: Sesame seed paste is available at Middle Eastern shops (or see
Appendix for mail-order sources).

Yield: 1¾ cups

TAHINI DIPPING SAUCE (SESAME SEED PASTE DIP)

½ cup tahini (see note below)

⅓–½ cup fresh lemon juice (depending on degree of tartness desired)

2 cloves garlic, quartered

1 cup water

1 teaspoon sugar

1 whole bunch parsley, stems removed

4 or 5 Calamata olives (or similar salted Mediterranean-style black olives) for garnish

1. Place tahini, lemon juice, garlic, water, and sugar in food processor container. Process until a coarse puree results, adding more water if needed to make a course paste that is fluid enough for dipping. Add parsley and process only enough to combine so green flecks of parsley remain in dish (If you don't have a food processor, simply chop everything fine and combine.)

2. Transfer to attractive serving dish and arrange 4 or 5 Calamata olives on top for garnish. This dish can also be garnished with toasted sesame seeds.

Note: Tahini (sesame seed paste) is commercially available at Middle Eastern shops and at some supermarkets. (See Appendix for mail-order sources.)

Yield: 1½ cups

YOGURT CHEESE DIP

2   cups plain yogurt
1   clove garlic, quartered
1   tablespoon olive oil
¼   teaspoon salt
¼   teaspoon freshly ground pepper
1   cucumber, peeled, seeded, chopped, then wrung out in a kitchen towel to extract as much liquid as possible
1   teaspoon fresh lemon juice
6   walnut halves for garnish

1. Lay a double thickness of cheesecloth or a thin piece of muslin in a colander so that the edges overlap and spoon yogurt into cheesecloth. Cover top of yogurt with edges of cloth. Set colander in a flat pan with raised sides and refrigerate for 6 to 24 hours. Yogurt will drain as it sits, getting thicker and thicker. (After 24 hours it will have shrunk to approximately half its original volume. The 1⅔ cup yield given below is based on 6 hours of draining time.) Discard liquid in pan under colander.

2. Place garlic, olive oil, salt, pepper, cucumber, and lemon juice in food processor and process until pureed. Remove from processor and stir in drained yogurt, mixing well. (If you have no food processor, simply chop everything and stir into drained yogurt.) Transfer to attractive serving bowl and garnish with walnut halves.

Yield: 1⅔ cups

SHRIMP WITH KA'EK AND ZA'TAR

Middle Easterners eat their ka'ek *(sesame-topped bread rings) in a fascinating way. They break off a piece of the* ka'ek, *then dip the torn edge of the bread into two small dishes—first into a bowl of good-quality olive oil, then into a flat dish filled with a spice mixture called* za'tar. *Za'tar is a greenish herb mixture that combines thyme, marjoram, and oregano, along with salt. The commercially sold* za'tar *mixtures also contain sesame seeds. You can make* za'tar *at home by mixing 2 tablespoons each of these ground herbs, then adding salt to taste along with a teaspoon or two of sesame seeds. Or you can buy the* za'tar *at any local Middle Eastern market. There's a reddish herb mixture that is also called* za'tar, *but this reddish mixture of thyme and sumac is not nearly as palatable for Westerners as is the greenish* za'tar. *For information on where to order* za'tar *by mail, see the Appendix.*

We have added grilled shrimp to this charming ritual. Dip the shrimp in the za'tar *and oil along with the* ka'ek. *We also suggest serving this as an appetizer. If you wish to serve it as a main dish, add at least one more type of Middle Eastern dip to serve along with the* za'tar. *In any case, serve glasses of icy cold beer with this dish.*

3 pounds shrimp, shelled and deveined
1 recipe Basic Marinade (see Index)
4 *ka'ek* yeast bread rings (see following recipe)
1 bowl extra-virgin olive oil
1 large flat dish filled with *za'tar*
   Oil for greasing grill

1. *Marinate shrimp:* Place shrimp in a plastic bag, pour marinade in to cover, and secure with twister seal. Turn bag several times to make sure that all shrimp surfaces touch the marinade. Place bag in a bowl and let sit at room temperature for 1 hour.

2. While shrimp marinates, place *ka'ek*, olive oil, and *za'tar* on dinner table.

3. *Grill shrimp:* At serving time, remove shrimp from marinade and place on prepared grill. Grill shrimp 2 to 3 minutes on each side or until they have lost their translucency and have a cooked appearance. Transfer to serving platter and bring to table immediately.

4. Show guests how to dip both the shrimp and the hunks of *ka'ek* first in the olive oil, then in the *za'tar*. Serve with cold beer or wine.

Yield: 4 servings

KA'EK (SESAME-TOPPED BREAD RINGS)

Ka'ek is a Middle Eastern bread that resembles French and Italian bread, except that it is baked in large, donutlike rings and sprinkled liberally with sesame seeds. In the Middle East, this bread is traditionally made by hand; so if you do not have a food processor, you can make ka'ek *by following any standard yeast bread directions for mixing yeast with water and sugar, then stirring in remaining ingredients and kneading until smooth and silky. The version we've worked out here uses the food processor, and the bread is mixed in half-recipe batches because it is hard for food processors to accommodate 4 cups of flour all at once. We have also added untraditional egg yolks because we like the added richness. If you are a strict traditionalist and wish to make the bread without the egg, simply add a few teaspoons of extra water to compensate. Remember, ingredients in the directions are given in half amounts for two batches.*

2   ¼-ounce packages dry yeast
1   tablespoon sugar
½   cup lukewarm water (just warm to the touch)
4   cups all-purpose flour
1   teaspoon salt
2   egg yolks
1   tablespoon oil
½   cup milk
¼   cup water

TOPPING
1   egg, lightly beaten
2–3 tablespoons sesame seeds

   1. Pour 1 package dry yeast into small bowl, add 1½ teaspoons sugar, then add ¼ cup lukewarm water and stir to combine. Let sit 5 to 10 minutes or until yeast becomes active.
   2. Place 2 cups flour and ½ teaspoon salt in food processor container and pulse once to combine. In a separate bowl, mix 1 egg yolk, 1½ teaspoons oil, ¼ cup milk, and 2 tablespoons water.
   3. Add yeast mixture to flour. Pulse two or three times to combine. Then turn on motor and pour egg yolk/milk mixture through feed tube.

Process until a smooth, silky dough is formed, then continue processing 45 seconds longer.

4. Remove dough from food processor container. Squeeze it a few times, then set aside for a moment.

5. Repeat steps, making a second batch of *ka'ek*. Squeeze both balls of dough together and knead a few times to combine.

6. Place ball of dough in a large, lightly oiled bowl. Cover loosely with a sheet of plastic wrap or place a dish towel over top of dough. Let rise in a warm place for about 45 minutes, until doubled in bulk.

7. Punch dough down, remove from bowl, and squeeze dough a few times. Divide dough into four equal portions (8 to 9 ounces each). Roll and squeeze each portion into a rope about 11 to 12 inches long. Form into a ring, overlapping the ends slightly. Use a few drops of water to act as glue between overlapped ends, pressing to seal. Cover dough loosely with dish towel or plastic wrap and place on a baking sheet that has been either well oiled or topped with a sheet of parchment paper.

8. Let rings sit in a warm place until doubled in bulk. Beat egg for topping and use an egg-dipped pastry brush to paint top and sides of one ring. Sprinkle ring with 1½ teaspoons of sesame seeds or more if desired. Repeat with remaining dough rings, egg, and sesame seeds.

9. Place baking sheet in a 400°F oven and immediately turn heat down to 350°F. Bake about 30 minutes or until tops of rings are golden brown and loaves sound hollow when tapped. Let cool on wire rack. Then transfer to plastic bag until ready to serve.

Yield: 4 sesame-topped bread rings

SNAILS

The snail has long been sought after by the French as a delicacy. It has a mild flavor and is usually served with sauces.

These univalve mollusks are usually not available fresh (unless you live in an area where edible varieties can be picked up on the beach). We feel this is just as well. The enormous amount of work needed to coax them out of their shells (according to some books, the process takes more than two days) and prepare them makes them less attractive in the fresh state. Hopefully, they'll be widely available to the general public as squid is now—cleaned and frozen—in a few more years. Meanwhile, canned snails, which we use in the following recipes, can be found in specialty food shops or ordered by mail (see Appendix). The canned flavor can be eliminated entirely by using any seafood marinade. Remember that canned snails are precooked and only have to be warmed before serving.

TO PREPARE CANNED SNAILS FOR GRILLING:

Remove snails from the can and place in a bowl, cover with water, allow to stand for one to two minutes, and drain.

GRILLED SNAILS ON ANGEL HAIR PASTA WITH WHITE WINE MARINADE

MARINADE

1	cup dry white wine
2	teaspoons crumbled dried basil
6	cloves garlic, minced
¼	teaspoon salt
¼	teaspoon freshly ground pepper
2	tablespoons melted butter

SHELLFISH

2	7½-ounce cans snails (about 36 snails per can), drained and rinsed
6	10-inch wooden skewers, soaked in cold water 30 minutes and drained

Oil for greasing grill

1. *Prepare marinade:* Combine marinade ingredients in a medium saucepan; add snails. Simmer 10 minutes, stirring often.
2. Divide snails among skewers.
3. Arrange skewers on prepared grill over ashen coals. Grill for 2 minutes, turn, and grill for 2 minutes longer. Brush with remaining marinade during grilling. Serve snails on a bed of angel hair pasta tossed with butter and crème fraîche (see Sea Scallops with Roe, served with Crème Fraîche and Freshwater Caviar; for directions for making crème fraîche).

Yield: 6 servings

GRILLED SNAILS MARINATED IN RED WINE WITH HERBES DE PROVENCE

MARINADE

1 cup dry red wine
2 teaspoons herbes de Provence
⅛ teaspoon salt
⅛ teaspoon freshly ground pepper
2 tablespoons butter, melted

SHELLFISH

2 7½-ounce cans snails (about 36 snails per can), drained
   and rinsed
6 10-inch wooden skewers, soaked in water 30 minutes
   and drained
Oil for greasing grill

1. *Prepare marinade:* Combine marinade ingredients in a medium saucepan. Bring marinade to a boil over medium heat, reduce heat to low, and simmer for 3 to 4 minutes. Add snails. Simmer 10 minutes, stirring often. Liquid will reduce until snails are just covered with marinade.
2. Divide snails among skewers.
3. *Grill snails:* Place on prepared grill over ashen coals. Grill for 2 minutes, turn, and grill for 2 minutes longer. Brush with remaining marinade during grilling. Serve on a bed of buttered spinach noodles.

Yield: 6 servings

SQUID

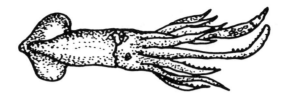

Except for baby squid, which are available fresh in most large cities, this univalve mollusk is largely available frozen. Medium-size squid (the kind called for in our stuffed squid recipes) and squid mantles are almost always frozen, and we have never seen squid steaks available in any state other than the frozen one. Luckily, frozen squid is absolutely delicious, especially when marinated before being grilled, and both frozen medium-size mantles and frozen steaks are fine for our recipes.

To use squid steaks, simply defrost and with a sharp knife or scissors cut into serving squares of equal size.

To use frozen squid mantles, rinse under cold running water, then run your finger inside to make sure mantle is absolutely clean. Although our recipes call for medium-size squid mantles, if you wish, you can substitute fresh baby squid mantles, which are often available. None of our stuffed squid mantle recipes make use of the tentacles, but if you wish to substitute fresh baby squid and clean them yourself, follow the directions below for cleaning fresh squid and using the tentacles.

TO CLEAN BABY OR MEDIUM-SIZE SQUID:

Separate the mantle (body) from the tentacles. To do this, hold the body in one hand and use the other hand to hold the tentacles just above the eyes. Gently pull the two sections apart. To clean the body portion, remove the transparent sword-shaped quill called the *pen*. This rudimentary bone is located in the back of the body. You'll be able to feel this tiny bone when you hold the body. Make a small cut at the top of the bony portion, then squeeze or pull the quill out and discard.

Next, take a spoon or use your finger and insert it into the mantle, scooping out any remaining matter. Rinse the body under cold running water and then peel off the outer membrane. The meat underneath will be snow white in color. Finally, pull the fins away from the body.

If you wish to use the tentacles in any of the stuffed squid recipes, clean them as follows: Cut the eye section away from the arms and discard the eyes. In the center of the tentacles, at the base, you'll feel a small, hard bone. This is the beak. Squeeze it out by applying pressure with both thumbs. When the tentacle portion is cleaned, chop it finely and brown it in a little butter; then add it to the stuffing you've made.

SQUID STEAKS WITH TAPENADE

Tapenade is a dark, pungent sauce from the south of France. It is always served cold or at room temperature.

SEAFOOD
2 pounds squid steaks
1 recipe Basic Marinade (see Index)
Oil for greasing grill
Black olives and capers for garnish (optional)

TAPENADE
1 6½-ounce can oil-packed tuna, well drained
1 2-ounce can flat anchovies, well drained
⅓ cup capers
⅔ cup medium pitted black olives
6 tablespoons fresh lemon juice
1 teaspoon freshly ground pepper
⅔ cup good-quality olive oil

1. *Marinate squid:* Cut squid into serving-size steaks and place in plastic bag. Pour marinade into bag and close with twister seal. Turn bag several times, making sure marinade touches all squid surfaces. Let squid marinate at room temperature for 1 hour.

2. *Prepare tapenade:* Place tuna, anchovies, capers, black olives, lemon juice, pepper, and olive oil in food processor container. Process to a coarse puree. Transfer to serving bowl.

3. *Grill squid:* Remove squid from marinade and place on prepared grill. Cook 3 to 4 minutes on each side. Transfer to serving platter and top each squid steak amply with tapenade. Garnish with additional olives and capers, if desired.

Yield: 4 servings

SQUID STEAKS AND GRILLED POTATO SKINS NACHOS

SEAFOOD
2   pounds squid steaks
1   recipe Basic Marinade (see Index)

NACHOS
4   whole baked Idaho potatoes, cooled and halved lengthwise
4   tablespoons melted butter
Garlic salt to taste
Oil for brushing outside of skins
½   pound sharp cheddar cheese, grated
¾   cup evaporated milk
4   fresh or canned jalapeño peppers, seeds removed, cut into thin strips

1. *Marinate squid:* Cut squid into serving portions and place in plastic bag. Pour marinade into bag and secure with twister seal. Turn bag several times, making sure that marinade touches all squid surfaces. Place in a bowl and let sit at room temperature for 1 hour.

2. Scoop out potato pulp from potato halves, leaving about ¼ to ½ inch of potato in skin. Paint inside of potatoes liberally with melted butter, then sprinkle them liberally with garlic salt. Brush outside with oil.

3. Place cheddar and evaporated milk in the top of a double boiler over simmering water and allow to melt. Place strips of jalapeño peppers in a small serving bowl.

4. *Grill potato skins and squid:* Place potato skins, skin side down, on grill for 4 minutes. Turn and cook another 4 minutes. Place squid on grill and cook 3 to 4 minutes on each side. Transfer to serving platter and serve quickly, spooning cheese over potatoes and squid, then sprinkling cheese liberally with jalapeño strips.

Yield: 4 servings

MARINATED SQUID STEAKS WITH BESSARA (MIDDLE EASTERN BEAN DIP WITH TA'LEYA TOPPING)

The following recipe uses a Middle Eastern bean puree called bessara *as a dip for chunks of grilled skewered squid.* Bessara *is made from broad fava beans (fava beans come in several sizes; use only the large, flat beans for this dish), which need 2 hours of preliminary simmering and 4 hours of soaking. The puree is garnished with thinly sliced onion rings and spoonfuls of a mixture of minced garlic and crushed coriander seed called* ta'leya, *which is sautéed for a few moments in olive oil. Fava beans are available at Middle Eastern markets or by mail order (see Appendix).*

SEAFOOD
2 pounds squid steaks
1 recipe Basic Marinade (see Index)
Oil for greasing grill

BESSARA
½ pound (8 ounces) broad fava beans
1 small onion, quartered
2 cloves garlic, peeled and quartered
2 tablespoons chopped fresh cilantro
1 teaspoon ground cumin
½ teaspoon salt
½ teaspoon dried mint
¼ teaspoon cayenne pepper
6 tablespoons cold water (or more if needed)
¼ cup good-quality olive oil

GARNISH
1 small onion, cut into paper-thin slices and separated
   into rings

TA'LEYA
2 tablespoons good-quality olive oil
3 cloves garlic, minced very fine
3 teaspoons ground coriander

1. *Prepare beans:* Soak fava beans in water to cover overnight. Then pick off any beans or debris floating on the surface of the water. Drain beans and place in a saucepan. Next morning, cover with water, heat to boil, and simmer 1½ to 2 hours, adding more water occasionally, until beans are fork-tender.

2. *Marinate squid:* Cut squid into serving-size steaks and place in plastic bag. Pour marinade into plastic bag and secure with twister seal. Turn bag several times to make certain that all sides of squid are exposed to marinade.

3. *Prepare bessara:* Place bessara ingredients in food processor. process for a moment. Then add drained beans and process again, pulsing several times, adding more water if necessary. Continue pulsing until a coarse puree results. Check consistency; the puree should be liquid enough to be scooped up on a piece of bread. If not, add water. Transfer puree to a flat serving dish with a lot of top surface and arrange onion rings decoratively over the top.

4. *Prepare* ta'leya: Heat oil in a small frying pan. Sauté garlic and coriander in oil for a few moments over low heat, stirring constantly with a wooden spoon and taking care that mixture does not burn. Use a rubber spatula to remove all *ta'leya* from pan and sprinkle over top of onion rings and *bessara.*

5. *Grill squid:* Remove squid steaks from marinade and place on prepared grill. Grill about 3 to 4 minutes on each side. Serve immediately, topped with bessara and onion rings.

Yield: 4 servings

SQUID STEAKS WITH CAPONATA

Caponata is a delicious Sicilian vegetable stew based on sweet and sour eggplant. It is traditionally served cold or at room temperature. But it's also delicious hot, as this recipe illustrates.

SEAFOOD

2   pounds squid steaks
1   recipe Basic Marinade (see Index)
Oil for greasing grill

CAPONATA

½   cup good-quality mild olive oil
1   pound eggplant (use baby eggplant if possible), cut into ¼-inch dice
1   large onion, minced fine
2   stalks celery, peeled thoroughly with vegetable peeler (make sure that all veins are removed) and chopped fine
1   green pepper, seeded, deveined, and chopped fine
1   red pepper, seeded, deveined, and chopped fine
1   1-pound can Italian tomatoes with liquid
2   tablespoons brown sugar
¼   cup red wine vinegar
½   teaspoon salt
1½ teaspoons freshly ground pepper
½   cup raisins
2   tablespoons capers
⅓   cup pitted green olives, quartered (pimiento-stuffed, if desired)
⅓   cup quartered pitted black olives
⅓   cup pine nuts

1. *Marinate squid:* Cut squid into serving-size steaks and place in a plastic bag. Place plastic bag in a bowl. Pour marinade into plastic bag and secure with twister seal. Turn bag a few times, making certain marinade comes into contact with all squid steak surfaces. Let sit at room temperature 1 hour in bowl, turning bag occasionally.

2. *Prepare caponata:* Heat oil in large, heavy-bottomed frying pan. Sauté eggplant, onion, celery, green and red peppers, and canned tomatoes with liquid for a moment, turning with wooden spoon. Then add brown sugar, wine vinegar, salt, pepper, raisins, capers, and green and black olives. Stir to combine. Simmer over low heat 20 minutes, stirring often.

3. While caponata simmers, toast pine nuts: Place pine nuts in a small frying pan and place over medium heat. Watch carefully, stirring occasionally with wooden spoon. As soon as nuts begin browning, stir constantly until they have been exposed to the heat on all sides. Then remove frying pan from heat. Spoon caponata into serving bowl. Sprinkle with toasted pine nuts for garnish.

4. *Grill squid:* Remove squid steaks from marinade and place on prepared grill. Grill steaks 2 to 3 minutes on each side. Transfer to heated serving platter. Serve each steak topped with a liberal portion of caponata and pass additional caponata.

Yield: 4 servings

SQUID CANNELLONI WITH TOMATO SAUCE

SEAFOOD

28 4-inch-long squid mantles, cleaned and tentacles
       discarded
Juice of 1 fresh lemon
¼ cup water

STUFFING

1   cup (8 ounces) ricotta cheese
6   tablespoons (3 ounces) finely chopped prosciutto
½   cup grated Parmesan cheese
¼   cup finely chopped fresh parsley
1   clove garlic, minced fine
¼   teaspoon salt
¼   teaspoon freshly ground pepper
Round wooden toothpicks for closing squid mantle
       openings

TOMATO SAUCE

2   tablespoons good-quality olive oil
6   large ripe tomatoes, peeled, seeded, and chopped
½   teaspoon salt
¼   teaspoon freshly ground pepper
1   bay leaf
Pinch dried basil
Oil for brushing squid and greasing grill

1. Check squid mantles with fingers (see the beginning of this chapter) to be sure that insides of mantles are clean. Place mantles in bowl and cover with lemon juice mixed with water. Let sit while you make the filling.

2. *Prepare stuffing:* Combine stuffing ingredients, mixing well. Stuff each squid mantle loosely with mixture, using only a scant tablespoon per mantle. Close openings with round wooden toothpicks.

3. *Prepare tomato sauce:* Heat oil in large heavy-bottomed frying pan. Add tomatoes, salt, pepper, bay leaf, and basil. Simmer 15 to 20 minutes over low heat, stirring occasionally with a wooden spoon.

4. *Grill squid:* When tomato sauce is done, brush stuffed squid mantles with oil and place on prepared grill. Cook about 2 to 3 minutes on each side. Serve immediately with hot tomato sauce.

Yield: 4 servings

SQUID STUFFED WITH GARLIC CRUMBS

This recipe calls for cleaned baby squid mantles, each about 4 inches long. Many fish stores thoroughly clean the mantles before selling. If your store does not, buy baby squid and follow the directions at the beginning of this chapter to clean them. In this recipe, the squid tentacles are not used.

SEAFOOD

28 4-inch-long squid mantles, cleaned and tentacles
    discarded
Juice of 1 fresh lemon
¼ cup water

STUFFING

1½ cups unseasoned commercial bread crumbs
3 cloves garlic, minced very fine
½ cup finely minced fresh parsley
¾ cup (1½ sticks) butter, melted
¾ teaspoon salt
¾ teaspoon freshly ground pepper
Round wooden toothpicks for closing squid mantle
    openings
Oil for brushing squid and greasing grill
Lime or lemon wedges for sprinkling on grilled squid

1. Open squid mantles and check to be sure insides are clean, using fingers. Mix lemon juice and water. Place squid in bowl and pour lemon juice mixture over squid, making sure that a little gets inside each mantle. Toss to combine and let sit.

2. *Prepare stuffing:* Combine crumbs, minced garlic, minced parsley, melted butter, salt, and pepper together in a bowl. Stuff squid mantles sparsely with crumb mixture, using a scant tablespoon of stuffing per squid mantle and taking care not to stuff any mantle too full.

3. Close mantle openings with round wooden toothpicks. If you are going to grill squid mantles immediately, brush with oil. Otherwise, place stuffed squid mantles on a plate, slip into a plastic bag, refrigerate for a few hours before serving, and then brush with oil.

4. *Grill squid:* Place squid on prepared grill and cook on each side for about 2 minutes, turning carefully with spatula. Serve immediately with lime or lemon wedges.

Yield: 4 servings

An assortment of grilled vegetables adds color and texture to your dinner plate. In addition to the following recipes we suggest you try grilling turnips, salsify, or okra. Use either the Basic Marinade (see Index) or the marinade in the Grilled Asparagus recipe in this chapter.

GRILLED ASPARAGUS

½ cup olive oil
3 tablespoons tarragon vinegar
3 tablespoons dried tarragon
3 tablespoons chopped onion
2 teaspoons chopped fresh chives
2 tablespoons chopped fresh parsley
¼ teaspoon salt
⅛ teaspoon freshly ground pepper
1½ pounds medium asparagus, tough ends snapped off
    and bottom third of asparagus peeled using vegetable
    peeler
Oil for greasing grill

1. *Prepare marinade:* Combine olive oil, vinegar, tarragon, onion, chives, parsley, salt, and pepper in a shallow glass bowl or in a glass pie plate.
2. Marinate asparagus for 20 to 30 minutes, turning once; drain.
3. Place asparagus horizontally on prepared grate so as to minimize loss into grill or arrange asparagus in a prepared grill basket. Grill vegetables 2 minutes on each side. Remove from grill and serve asparagus hot.

Yield: 6 servings

MIDDLE EASTERN GRILLED VEGETABLES

1   medium eggplant, cut into thick (½- to ⅔-inch) slices
Salt
1   large green pepper, seeded, deveined, and cut into
    lengthwise quarters
1   large red pepper, seeded, deveined, and cut into
    lengthwise quarters
1   large onion, cut into ⅓-inch slices
1   recipe Basic Marinade (see Index)
1   tablespoon sesame seeds
Oil for greasing grill

1. Lay eggplant slices in a single layer on paper towels and lightly salt them on both sides. Let sit 30 minutes or until enough bitter juices have run out of eggplant slices to discolor the paper towels.

2. *Marinate vegetables:* Place eggplant, green and red pepper quarters, and onion slices in plastic bag. Pour marinade over vegetables into bag and secure with twister seal. Turn bag several times, making sure vegetable surfaces touch marinade. Place bag in bowl and let sit at room temperature 1 hour, turning bag several times.

3. While vegetables marinate, toast sesame seeds: Place in a single layer in a small heavy-bottomed frying pan and set over medium heat. Watch carefully, stirring occasionally with wooden spoon. As soon as they begin to brown, give them your full attention. Let frying pan remain on the heat for a few more seconds, then remove pan. Seeds will continue to darken slightly after being removed from heat. When cool, transfer to small dish and reserve for sprinkling on grilled vegetables.

4. Lay individual vegetable slices and pieces on prepared grill in a single layer and let cook for 4 to 5 minutes on each side or until vegetables are browned. Since eggplant is more delicate than either onions or peppers, it may have to be taken off the grill earlier than the other vegetables. Serve immediately, sprinkled with sesame seeds if desired.

Yield: 4 servings

DOUBLE SQUASH GRILL

2   butternut squash
2   acorn squash
¼   pound (1 stick) butter at room temperature
1   teaspoon honey
½   teaspoon ground ginger
¼   cup firmly packed light brown sugar
Oil for greasing grill

1. *Prepare squash:* Cut squash into ½- to ¾-inch slices; discard ends. Remove and discard fibers and seeds from squash.

2. Cut butter into small pieces and mix well in food processor fitted with steel blade. Add honey, ginger, and brown sugar and blend.

3. Brush honey butter over squash rounds. Arrange squash on paper toweling in microwave and process for 4 minutes on high.

4. When ready to grill, arrange squash on prepared grill over medium-hot coals. Brush with butter and grill for 2 to 4 minutes: turn over. Grill for 1 to 2 minutes or until tender. Serve hot. Squash will char, making it very attractive. Serve with extra honey butter.

Yield: 4–6 servings

BREADED EGGPLANT SLICES ON THE GRILL

1   large eggplant (at least 1 pound)
Salt
2   eggs
1   tablespoon snipped fresh chives
¼   teaspoon salt
1½ cups very fine bread crumbs (use commercial crumbs
     if possible, as they are very fine)
½   cup finely grated Parmesan or Romano cheese
¼   teaspoon salt
1   teaspoon freshly ground pepper

1. Wash and dry eggplant. Peel eggplant with vegetable peeler if desired or leave skin on. Cut into scant ½-inch slices and arrange then in a single layer on paper towels. Sprinkle both sides lightly with salt. Let sit at room temperature 30 minutes or until some of the bitter juice has discolored the paper.

2. Meanwhile, combine eggs, chives, and ¼ teaspoon salt in a medium bowl. Then combine bread crumbs, grated cheese, ¼ teaspoon salt, and pepper in a second bowl.

3. Dry both sides of eggplant slices with paper towels. Dip slices, one at a time, into egg/chive mixture, then into bread crumb/grated cheese mixture. Arrange coated slices in an individual layer on a flat plate and refrigerate for at least 1 hour before putting on the grill.

4. Lay eggplant slices on the grill and grill 4 to 5 minutes on each side, using spatula to turn.

Yield: 4 servings

MINIATURE VEGETABLES ON THE GRILL: PATTYPAN SQUASH, ZUCCHINI WITH BLOSSOMS

¼ pound cheddar cheese, cut into slivers
¾ pound zucchini with blossoms, if possible
¾ pound miniature pattypan squash
Oil for brushing vegetables and grill
Salt and freshly ground pepper
½ cup bay leaves

1. *Grill vegetables:* Insert cheese slivers into zucchini blossoms. Brush zucchini and squash with oil. Arrange vegetables on prepared grill, making sure that zucchini are perpendicular to grate. Sprinkle vegetables with salt and pepper to taste.

2. Arrange about 6 bay leaves over vegetables. Slip remaining bay leaves through the grate so they will burn, releasing their flavor on vegetables.

3. Grill vegetables for 2 minutes; brush with oil. Turn over carefully and cook for 2 minutes or until done. Serve hot.

Yield: 6 servings

GRILLED GARLIC BREAD

3 cloves garlic, minced fine
1 tablespoon good-quality olive oil
¼ pound (1 stick) butter, melted
8 thick slices Italian or French bread

1. *Prepare garlic bread:* Fry garlic in hot olive oil over medium-low heat until golden in color.
2. Stir in butter. Brush bread on both sides with butter mixture.
3. Place garlic bread on prepared grill and cook for 1 minute. Brush again with butter-garlic mixture and grill for 1 minute longer or to taste. Watch carefully to be sure bread does not burn. Remove from grill and serve.

Yield: 6–8 servings

CROSTINI (SKEWERED BREAD AND CHEESE)

This dish is an American version of a classic Italian dish called crostini. *It consists of skewered hunks of bread and Provaturo cheese. If you can't find Provaturo, substitute provolone or any cheese of equal firmness. The nontraditional egg-breadcrumb topping for the cheese chunks prevents it from melting off of the skewers as quickly as it would if unprotected. Crostini is traditionally served with an anchovy sauce such as the bagna cauda that accompanies shrimp (see Index). But it will go well with almost any strongly flavored sauce in this book.*

1 pound provolone or other natural cheese of similar hardness
2 eggs
2 cups fine bread crumbs
$\frac{1}{8}$ teaspoon salt
2 pinches cayenne pepper
1 loaf French bread, torn into $1\frac{1}{2}$-inch chunks (do not remove crust)
4 skewers
$\frac{1}{2}$ cup melted butter
Garlic salt
Oil for greasing grill

1. Cut cheese into scant $\frac{1}{2}$-inch-thick pieces, each about 1 inch high and 1 inch wide. Beat eggs until well mixed. Combine bread crumbs, salt, and cayenne pepper in a flat dish.
2. Dip cheese chunks in beaten eggs, then roll each in bread crumbs. Thread bread and cheese alternately on skewers, making sure that bread hunks are substantially larger than cheese chunks.
3. Brush skewered bread and cheese with a pastry brush dipped in melted butter on all sides. Then sprinkle garlic salt liberally on all sides of skewers.
4. Lay skewers on prepared grill for a moment or two or until cheese begins to melt and the edges of the bread begin to brown. Turn skewers and watch carefully for another moment or two. Remove skewers from grill as soon as cheese is soft but retains enough body to cling to skewers.

Yield: 4 servings

GRILLED ORANGE SLICES

2   large seedless navel oranges
½   cup port (use only real port from Portugal)
¼   cup honey
Oil for greasing grill

1. Rinse whole, unpeeled oranges under running water. Heat a medium-size pot of water to boiling, then slip whole oranges into water. Boil for 30 minutes. Pour off boiling water and place pot containing oranges under cold running water until cool enough to handle.

2. Meanwhile, combine port and honey in a small bowl. Cut whole oranges (do not remove rinds) into thick (larger than ½ inch) slices and place in plastic bag. Place bag in bowl. Pour port/honey mixture over oranges. Secure bag with twister seal and turn several times, making sure cut orange surfaces touch marinade. Let sit at room temperature 1 hour or more, turning bag occasionally.

3. When ready to cook, place orange slices on heated, well-oiled grill and cook 3 to 4 minutes or until oranges are lightly browned on edges. Grill marks should be apparent. Turn oranges and repeat on remaining side. Serve immediately, spooning a little of remaining marinade over each if desired.

Yield: 4 servings

APPENDIX:
MAIL-ORDER SOURCES OF INGREDIENTS

The Chef's Catalog
3215 Commercial Ave.
Northbrook, IL 60062
(312) 480-9400
  Grill basket.

Carolyn Collins Caviar
PO Box 662
Crystal Lake, IL 60014
(815) 459-6210
  Freshwater caviar.

Food Stuffs
338 Park Ave.
Glencoe, IL 60022
(312) 835-5105
  Canned snails.

Holy Land Grocery, Inc.
4806 N. Kedzie Ave.
Chicago, IL 60659
(312) 588-3306
  Tahini, za'tar (specify green,
not red), and broad fava beans.

The Oriental Food Market
2801 W. Howard St.
Chicago, IL 60645
(312) 274-2826
  Black beans, Oriental wooden
barbecue skewers, Oriental
sesame oil, shrimp paste, and
nam pla (Thai bottled fish sauce).

Star Market
3349 N. Clark St.
Chicago, IL 60659
(312) 472-0599
  Japanese soy sauce.

Wild Game, Inc.
1941 W. Division St.
Chicago, IL 60622
(312) 278-1661
  Shiitake mushrooms.

INDEX